The University of Worcester

AN ILLUSTRATED HISTORY

The University of Worcester

AN ILLUSTRATED HISTORY

Paul Cheeseright

THE UNIVERSITY OF WORCESTER:
AN ILLUSTRATED HISTORY

Copyright © University of Worcester

First published in 2008
by James & James (Publishers) Limited, a member of
the Third Millennium Information Limited Group

2–5 Benjamin Street
London
United Kingdom
EC1M 5QL
www.tmiltd.com

ISBN: 978 1 903942 81 9

British Library Cataloguing in Publication Data
A CIP catalogue record for this book is available from
the British Library.

Project editor: Susan Millership
Picture research: Susan Millership
Designer: Susan Pugsley
Production manager: Bonnie Murray

Reprographics by Asia Graphic Printing Ltd
Printed by Gorenjski Tisk, Slovenia

*Endpaper: detail of students and staff at City
of Worcester Training College, 1946–47.*

Contents

FOREWORD

BY JOHN YELLAND, PRESIDENT OF THE
UNIVERSITY'S COLLEGE OF FELLOWS AND
CHAIR OF THE BOARD OF GOVERNORS
1999–2007

How proud we are that our cathedral city of Worcester now boasts a fully fledged university – the University of Worcester. As the only higher education institution in the counties of Hereford and Worcestershire and currently the fastest growing university in the country, the University of Worcester is playing a major part in the creation of a vibrant regional economy and society.

This book charts the long, at times demanding, road that the University has walked during its first six decades. From its early days as a post-war teacher training college, operating from 'temporary' former Air Ministry buildings, some of which still serve as offices to this day, via the radical changes to higher education as a whole in 1992, to achieving the crowning accolade of full university title in 2005, the history of the University of Worcester is a rich and colourful one.

From the beginning, Worcester has been famed for the excellence of its teacher training. Over the years, the University has successfully expanded the range and variety of its courses. We now provide excellent opportunities in business, sports science, the humanities and creative arts, as well as in education. Science facilities include the country's National Pollen and Aerobiology Research Unit and the University has been providing first class pre and post registration education and training in nursing and midwifery since 1995.

The most recent chapter in the history of the University of Worcester has been its determined project to create a new campus in the heart of the city. The historic former site of the Worcester Royal Infirmary has been chosen for this exciting, vitally

Opposite: Woodcut by Anne Skinner from the College magazine, 1950.

important venture. The British Medical Association was founded in the Infirmary's original Georgian building and the hospital's Jenny Lind Chapel is one of Worcester's most beautiful Victorian buildings. The University will respect the site's wonderful historic buildings and give them a new purpose for the future. The City Campus will allow the University to integrate still further with Worcester life, benefiting students, the community and businesses alike.

The history of our University is one of exciting achievements, none of which would have been attained without the hard work, inspiration and devotion of the staff. It is the staff and students together who create the friendly, constructive, professional atmosphere for which Worcester is renowned.

I would like to thank all those who helped to bring together our story in this volume, particularly the University's alumni and many friends in the City and wider region. I commend this book to you.

May 2008

ACKNOWLEDGEMENTS

Goodwill and cooperation have been constant companions during the preparation of this book. I am indebted to many people at the University and its predecessor colleges, to others in and around the City, for their time and recollections, for their insights and information, and for immense good cheer in smoothing my journey.

I am especially grateful to Helen and Iain Ball, Dick Bryant, Jackie Clarke, Rod Coveney, Pat Finch, David Green, Mike Grundy, David Hallmark, Sian Hobday, Philip Hytch, Helen Johnstone, Wendy Logan, Doreen Milton, Chris Neumeier, John Nixon, Grace Peirson, Kathy Preece, Mike Pryce, John Ryan, Pam Stubbs, Val Williams, Xie Yuan Hui and John Yelland.

At James & James, Hamish MacGibbon deftly and encouragingly guided the project, while Susan Millership, with Susan Pugsley and Bonnie Murray, brought sensitive skill and flair to production of the book. Alison Thomas edited the copy with a mixture of delicacy and rigour.

Five chapter headings come from two volumes of poetry by Lawrence Binyon. *Autumn Song*, from a collection called *The North Star*, published by Macmillan (London, 1941), provided the title for Chapter Five. The titles for Chapters Two, Three, Four and Six came respectively from *The Cherry Trees*, *The Orchard*, *The Burning of the Leaves* and *The Winds of all the World*, all of which are in the collection, *The Burning of the Leaves*, again published by Macmillan (London, 1944).

Paul Cheeseright.

Chapter One

SABRINA

Sabrina gazes, wide-eyed, from the coat of arms of the University of Worcester. A mythological figure, daughter of Estrildis and Locrine, who gave her name to the river Severn after being drowned in it, Sabrina supervises the University's geographical roots.

The University of Worcester's coat of arms, presided over by Sabrina, a mythological figure who gave her name to the River Severn. The wavy lines on the crest represent the river.

Opposite: The Severn at Worcester by W.R. Lane from the College magazine, 1954.

Worcester Cathedral by John O'Connor, 1886.

The wavy lines on the crest are the Severn. The bulrushes and swans span the river, explaining its importance to the city, and alluding to the original University campus on the west side and the new campus on the east, city side. The Severn also links the University with its hinterland and tells the world that this is an institution not merely for the city, but for the entire region.

Sabrina is also a reminder of the shared lineage of the University and the city with Worcester Cathedral. From this lineage, historical circles can be discerned, as the past finds an echo in the activities of the present.

What is now Worcester Cathedral has been a site of prayer and worship since the seventh century. During the ninth century, King Alfred sent the Bishop of Worcester a training manual which urged the clergy to translate books from Latin into English, so that local people could learn to read in their indigenous language. Here was an early example of the policy of widening participation in learning, precisely the course followed by the 21st century University. The service to celebrate the granting of a university title to Worcester took place in the cathedral, where the University now formally awards its degrees. Ancient learning has strong links with contemporary education. But there is yet another historical circle. The present cathedral dates back to the 11th century, when it was a Benedictine priory. Worcester College, part of the University of Oxford, has the same Benedictine origin. First known as Gloucester Hall, it became

Worcester College only after a bequest from a Worcestershire landowner in 1714. College and University were brought together in 2005, when Worcester College, Oxford gave its approval to the use of the name 'University of Worcester'.

The wide circles spanning the centuries became tighter after 1946. The long tradition of general and spiritual learning associated with the cathedral's thousand-year history became more closely directed – even political.

When David Green, Vice Chancellor of the new University, spoke at the formal opening during 2006, he alluded to the trend of a more applied vocational curriculum, as opposed to a concentration on the liberal arts. This took the University back to the philosophy of the original teachers training college: none of the students would have been there had they not wished to pursue that particular vocation.

Similarly, Green looked to the surroundings, making it clear that one of the principal functions of the new University would be to make a ready source of learning and opportunity available to people outside the urban centres. When returned servicemen and women came to the College in the late 1940s, one of the areas singled out for special training was Rural Studies. Since then, only the educational techniques have changed; the concern behind them remains the same.

Rural Studies was important at Worcester, at least in part, because the government of the day made it so. This points to a general trend since the immediate post-war period. The University (and the colleges before it) are the children of official policy. Consequently, they have surfed on a historical tide: starting as a response to the expansion of schooling; developing as the tertiary educational system grew after the Robbins report in the 1960s; and expanding further as government policy sought to bring more and more young people into the system and provide them with tools to cope in the outside world. But the children are no longer naive youngsters. The University is a mature adult institution; its independence has grown and continues to develop. Green enjoys a freedom of action denied to his predecessors.

Securing this independence has not been easy. The historical tide was frequently choppy: policy may have been consistent in its widest sense, but it has been disturbed by economic and electoral circumstances. How the Principals and their colleagues at Worcester responded is outlined in the following account.

Detail from the Beauchamp tomb in Worcester Cathedral.

Next page: Cricket in the shadow of Worcester Cathedral.

Chapter Two

HOPE THAT BLOSSOMS IN THE HEART

HINES, 1946–51

The telegram from Worcester read 'chaotic but promising'. Fred Grice had cautiously left his wife at home in Durham, not knowing what he would find when he went to join the staff at a new college on an old estate just west of Worcester city centre. Had he known, he might have been deterred. There was no welcome: rather an elderly Royal Air Force watchman greeted him at the gate as if he should not have been there at all. He had to find his own bed, which, he recalled later in the College magazine, had the appearance of one that you might 'expect to see in one of the more disreputable transit camps', with a pillow which 'resembled a sandbag that had missed its proper destiny'.

For all that, the succinct summary of prospects provided for his wife in the telegram sent after a few hours on the putative campus at Henwick Grove, proved to be accurate on the first count and prescient on the second. Chaotic the conditions at Henwick Grove certainly were, as helter-skelter local administration tried to catch up with events, and a weary nation tried to settle on a new equilibrium immediately after the end of the Second World War. To find his first sight of Worcester 'promising' made Grice an optimist: there was little at Henwick Grove to suggest an educational institution. The site was well placed on the edge of a cathedral city, and, at

Opposite: Henwick Grove by P.N.L. from the College magazine, 1951.

more than 50 acres, there was plenty of space, but the grounds were scruffy where there were no undercrops, and there was a stately home and three groups of single-storey Air Ministry buildings, the latter constructed for wartime purposes. The college was waiting to be made.

Grice and his colleagues may have had no time to ponder the broader significance of their presence in Worcester. In fact, they had a role in a national programme of major social change, and they played out that role on a site with its own educational and literary antecedents.

Ellen Wilkinson became Minister of Education in the Labour Government elected in 1945. She had a deep commitment to bringing into force the 1944 Butler Act – legislation carefully negotiated within the wartime coalition to transform the British school system. It provided for free nursery education and sought to make free secondary education available to all up to a new school-leaving age of 15. She faced the immediate problem that the educational system had run down during the war; there were not enough schools and insufficient teachers to cope with expansion. She responded with the Hutting Operation for the Raising of the School-leaving Age, and the Emergency Training Scheme for teachers. Henwick Grove, Worcester, fitted into the second scheme: Worcester Emergency Teachers Training College became one of 55 set up by the Ministry.

So it was that the 45-year-old Henry Hines, known as H.J., came to Worcester from the Canterbury Technical Institute, as the first principal of the nascent College. Early in 1946, he started work in a back room of the City of Worcester's Education Authority, with little more than a table, a chair and some writing materials. He needed staff, teaching equipment and the liberation of Henwick Grove from the Air Ministry and other government

Three early images of the campus taken between 1946 and 1948 showing Air Ministry buildings and Henwick Grove house, bequeathed to Worcester City Council by Gulielma Binyon for educational purposes.

Modern aerial view of the city with the St John's campus top left.

departments working there. He would be the first to assume responsibility for a property destined for education.

In 1861, Henwick Grove had become the family home of the Binyons, purchased by Thomas Binyon for his retirement, following a lucrative career as a Manchester cotton manufacturer and a tea and coffee merchant. By the 1920s the only survivor of Thomas's wing of the Binyon family was the spinster Gulielma. She was the cousin of Laurence Binyon, the poet and oriental scholar, recalled on Remembrance Sunday for his memorial to the fallen of the First World War: 'They shall grow not old, as we that are left grow old; / Age shall not weary them, nor the years condemn ...'

Laurence Binyon, friend and collaborator of the composer Edward Elgar, son of Worcester, first went to Henwick Grove as a boy, and continued to visit until Gulielma's death in 1942. He is part of the cultural prologue of the educational institution which took shape at Henwick Grove. So too is Gulielma, but in a different way. As local historian and journalist Mike Grundy explains, 'In her will, Miss Binyon offered Henwick Grove for sale at a nominal sum to Worcester City Council, apparently for education purposes... [and] the City Council took up the offer of the purchase.'

Hines had little time for historical legacies. Lecturers began to arrive in mid April 1946, but they had to sweep the floor before starting a staff meeting. According to records of staff meetings, discussion on the syllabus was 'adjourned so that the male lecturers might remove wardrobes'. On 30 April, the matron of the new college reported that 200 beds still had to be made up, 'and the female lecturers withdrew for the purpose'. Three days later, one of the residential blocks was flooded when the central heating was turned on before all the radiators were connected to the system. The day before the first students arrived (6 May) some floors had still not been washed, and Hines said that the lecturers would have to clean up.

This fevered activity took place in the three angular and solid single-storey blocks, each comprising a long central base, with spurs jutting out – barracks by any other name. They became the centre of the College, the living and working quarters. To these buildings came 240 demobilised servicemen and women, returning from around the globe, mature, war-wise people with backgrounds in 'travel, experience of affairs, participation in some form of social service', just as specified in the White Paper preceding the Butler Act. For many, the opportunity to undertake teacher training provided the step on to the professional ladder which they had been denied by the war years. It was a second chance, never mind that at the

H. J. HINES, M.Sc.
Principal
CITY OF WORCESTER
TRAINING COLLEGE

Cartoon from College magazine drawn by Thomas Goodman, one of the first students who went on to become an art teacher, 1947.

start, as Grice recollected a decade later, 'the college had a name, but it had next to no books, no badge, no colours, no labs to speak of'. Many of the students were as old as, or older than, Hines's newly recruited staff, but this was not a handicap. Because there was so little at the College to begin with, staff and students had to create an educational institution. Five months after the students arrived, Hines wrote that it had been 'an interesting experience watching this college come to life'.

Henry Hines, the first Principal, 1946–50.

City of Worcester Training College

Official
OPENING
July
13th
1946

Mr J. HINES
M.Sc.
Principal

Alderman
FRANK
BULLOCK J.P.

The Opener
Sir
PHILIP MORRIS
C.B.E.   M.A.

A TUTOR

A TUTOR

A TUTOR

TWO (very shy) TUTORS

Mr
K. GRAHAM
College
President.

Opposite: Official opening cartoons drawn by Thomas Goodman. Sir Philip Morris, in his opening speech, stressed that education should be 'fun first'.

An illustration incorporating the College Crest and the motto 'Aspire to Inspire' appeared on the front of the programme for the first 'Going Down' dinner, 1947. The interlinked hands reflect the 'Worcester spirit' of friendship and collaboration.

In fact, Hines did not simply watch: he set the tone. He was wise enough to recognise that demobilised servicemen and women had no desire to exchange one type of hierarchical discipline for another; and he had the sensitivity to appreciate that the enthusiasm of both staff and students for some normality in civilian life required freedom. Out of this awareness he evolved a regime of comradeship. 'Not the least happy of the characteristics of this college is the complete absence of rules and regulations imposed from above... ours is a healthy democracy', wrote K.M. Graham, president of the College Committee, the body which brought staff and students together. Watching what was going on from the College offices, Doreen Milton (née Crowsley), one of the first employees, remembered that 'Mr Hines was never remote from the students. He treated them as equals.'

Conditions in Britain during 1946 and 1947 – food rationing (Doreen Milton remembered clipping the ration books), limited transport, and so on – matched the lack of amenities in the College. This forced staff and students in on themselves. In their little residential community, they could be miserable together or happy together. Hines made certain it was the latter. Indeed, there was much talk of happiness. When Sir Philip Morris, Vice Chancellor of Bristol University, formally opened the College on one of the hottest days in the summer of 1946, he urged the students not to take themselves too seriously: education, he asserted, should be 'fun first'. George Tomlinson, who followed Ellen Wilkinson at the Ministry of Education, came to the College's first Presentation Day nearly a year later, and said he was pleased to see that happiness was the keynote of the

College. Chiming with Morris, he argued that there could be no education without happiness, and Hines, on the same occasion, claimed that happiness had been the feature throughout the year. Indeed, it was the mixture of happiness, internal democracy and enthusiasm that led to what became known as 'the Worcester spirit', a term frequently used in the 1950s and 1960s as an injunction to co-operative behaviour, but rarely heard in the 21st century, although some elements of this spirit remain in the much larger new University.

It would be inaccurate to see the College as simply an amiable exercise in collective living. Its purpose was serious and Hines was a serious and experienced educator. The notion of turning out brand new teachers in a year was a tall order. According to Hines, the committee which devised the scheme must have been appalled at its own temerity. In spite of this, according to official figures, the nationwide scheme produced 35,000 teachers, recruited from among ex-servicemen, women and people in industry and commerce. Of

Scenes from the official opening of the College, 1946.
From left to right: Mr Turnbull (Art), Mr Lovat (Geography)
and Mr Grice (English). The Principal, Mr Hines, centre,
with guests.

these, 234 passed out from Worcester. Each college had to ensure that the new teachers possessed a grounding in the subjects they would teach and a knowledge of educational techniques – what to do in the classroom. By 1948, the emergency scheme had started to wind down, and in October, emergency students accounted for just half of the new student roll.

By this time, the College had moved on to a more orthodox footing and had become part of the country's formal academic structure. In February 1948, Worcester City Council had accepted the invitation from the Ministry of Education to make

CITY OF WORCESTER
TRAINING COLLEGE

Opening Ceremony
SATURDAY, JULY 13th, 1946

Front cover of the City of Worcester
College Opening Ceremony pamphlet.

Scene from the student production of Macbeth *produced by Mary Cannell and staged in the Co-operative Hall, Worcester, 1948.*

the temporary arrangements permanent: to set up a teachers training college. In June of the same year, Worcester became one of ten West Midlands institutions admitted as a constituent college of the Institute of Education at Birmingham University – 'a very important stage in our history has begun', noted Hines. It meant that students passing out of what had now become the City of Worcester Training College (the first of several name changes over the decades) would have a qualification certified by Birmingham University, which represented a rise in status. It meant too that the College would offer two-year courses leading to the standard qualification for teachers, the Certificate of Education – no more rushed, emergency training. The first 128 students seeking the Certificate started work in October 1948. But there was also a niche in the academic system which the Ministry of Education was anxious that Worcester should fill.

This niche was Rural Studies. The geographical position of the College, close to the river Severn, surrounded by the Worcestershire and Herefordshire countryside, presented an obvious opportunity for the College to cater specifically for the needs of rural schools. The extent of the College's land, much of it already in agricultural use, allowed the development of a farm for training purposes: in those days, teachers in rural schools needed knowledge not only of the usual academic subjects, but also of tasks ranging from milking cows to swaddling babies. The government wanted a department at Worcester to provide a three-year course for domestic science students likely to become teachers in rural schools. Here was the genesis of the longstanding commitment of the College (and, subsequently, the University) to establishing the link between the educational institution and the rural community.

As the College settled down after the frenzy of the first emergency years, the facilities at Henwick Grove began to improve. While the accommodation remained shoddy, a new sports ground and gymnasium appeared and the College took possession of the farm buildings at Henwick House, the old Binyon residence. By September 1949, the last of the emergency students had departed and some 700 students had passed through Henwick Grove in three years. 'Possibly the most notable quality of the early days was the sense of urgency which was felt everywhere. This has, I believe, been maintained throughout the three years', Hines told readers of the College magazine.

Whether this sense of urgency would continue, Hines would never know. He had been ill during 1949, but even as he approached death in December 1950, his devotion to the College remained such that he fussed about whether Christmas festivities would go ahead: they must, he said; he wanted gaiety, not grimness. After his death, tributes flowed in with a generosity of sentiment beyond customary politeness. And they continued. Alan Gibbie, a second-year student in 1952, observed, 'This College was fashioned by Mr Hines, who worked himself to death for it.' Hines brought to his post an ideal of social democracy in action. 'The College would be a place where maximum freedom would be granted, where regulations would be conspicuous by their scarcity, and yet where responsible behaviour would be found and where each individual would make the best use of his talents and contribute his utmost to the common good,' wrote Cyril Ward, his Vice Principal. For a few years, Hines achieved what he wanted. His successors would find life more complicated.

Feeding chickens on the College farm.

Mary Cannell, back centre, and compa[...] take a boating trip on the River Severn

Students reading notices and mail, 1948.

The dining hall, 1948. Most students had served in the Second World War and were anxious to make up for lost time. Hines remarked that probably the most notable quality of the early days was the 'sense of urgency'.

Next page: Students on the campus today.

Chapter Three

WE HAVE PLANTED FOR DAYS TO COME

PEIRSON: 1951–62

'The Principal introduced himself', ran the first entry recorded in the handwritten minutes of the first staff meeting for a new era of the training college's history. The Principal wrote the minutes himself. His first announcement was that 'the college photograph would be taken on Monday 24 September at 12 noon'. E.G. Peirson, known as Ned, had picked up the reins from H.J. Hines. Staff meetings, he declared, would be formalised: they would take place on the first and last days of each term and minutes would be taken. It was an early sign that Hines's freewheeling style would be replaced by tighter organisation.

Peirson, a wartime major in the Royal Electrical and Mechanical Engineers, had come from Westminster College, where he had been head of mathematics. He found what he called 'a flourishing community of 300 students and 30 teaching staff with well-established traditions and an adventurous spirit working with tremendous enthusiasm'. He had no desire to change any of that and he fostered the freedom which gave students the opportunity 'to order their own lives' and to mix freely with staff. But he stayed within limits at once typical of residential educational institutions in the 1950s, and fitting for a man who practiced as a Methodist lay preacher (although he pushed his Methodism aside in later years).

Opposite: Woodcut showing aspects of rural studies by Ella Hunt from the College magazine, 1952.

E.G. Peirson (Ned), Principal, 1951–1978.

Worcester had been a mixed college from the outset, but in 1953 Peirson reminded members of staff that there could be no mixed parties in rooms after 10 pm and that permission for students to be out after 11 pm had to be obtained from the Principal or a senior member of staff. All the students had a personal tutor and formed groups around him or her; these personal groups met once a week, but Peirson noticed that some groups had a habit of meeting in residential rooms. 'As we have a rule that mixed parties should not be in residential rooms before 12.30 pm I should like this practice to cease', he told staff in April 1955. The College, in short, might be a happy, even a cosy, community in an agreeable semi-rural location, but it was not a louche country house party.

Certainly, Peirson struck the right tone from the official point of view. The government's inspectorate scrutinised the College and its work in 1956. The inspectors paid tribute to Hines and 'his understanding of how an adult community might grow', and went on to report that 'the present Principal, appointed in 1951, quickly appreciated the need for quiet growth and consolidation during the next few years, and has identified himself creatively with many of the aims of his predecessor'.

Peirson later looked back on the years between 1951 and 1957 as a period of consolidation, helped by the facts that the student body remained constant at around 320 and the staff was stable. The consolidation was visible in two ways: first, on the Henwick Grove site, and second, in the College's primary task of training teachers.

In order that the College be deemed permanent, it had to regain control of its property, which had been requisitioned during the Second World War, and which at that stage was leased from the Ministry of Works for £8,800 a year. The first stage came when the College assumed responsibility for the maintenance of the buildings during 1952, but it took a further two years before the purchase could be arranged, and then only after the intervention of the local Member of Parliament. The City of Worcester agreed to the purchase at the district valuer's valuation of £85,000 for the freehold and buildings. But it was not quite so simple. The Ministry of Education agreed to reimburse the city so that the transaction, as Worcester's *Evening News and Times* put it in an editorial, was 'somewhat out of the ordinary', but at least ratepayers would have

Valentine's Day dance, 1957.

no cause for worry: 'one government department will, in effect, pay over a sum of money to another'. Still, with the title to the land and buildings back with the city, Gulielma Binyon's intention would at last be honoured.

Settlement of this issue allowed Peirson to start planning for the future, but this was not straightforward. The settlement came with its own restrictions, and it quickly became obvious that the Ministry of Education had little taste for further extensive capital expenditure. Discussions with officials revealed that the Ministry thought that the wartime buildings, assumed to be temporary structures, would have a life of 30 years, subject to roof repairs and normal maintenance; the College ought to stay in them long enough to justify the purchase price. The Ministry estimate turned out to be too modest, as two of the three buildings which existed then remained in use into the 21st century, still solid, still squat. But in 1954, Peirson had to accept that there would be no new permanent buildings in the foreseeable future, although there would be agreed improvements to extend the dining facilities, along with teaching and living accommodation.

21st birthday party, 1956.

The second element of consolidation related to teacher training. The work to equip students with the Certificate of Education had bedded down quickly in the late 1940s, and by the mid 1950s, the reputation of the College had spread far enough for students to be drawn not only from the West Midlands, but from the country at large. One student, Iain Ball (1956–8), recalled how 'The College was established as being good – you'd be told "you'd be lucky if you get into Worcester"'. Indeed, the year before Ball arrived there had been 1,000 applications for 120 vacancies. With entry figures looking secure, consolidation thus involved the effort to improve what the students were offered.

The first 15 students taking the three-year course in domestic science, directed at work in rural schools, passed out in 1952. By that time, the position of the College as a rural studies centre had been enhanced to the point that it was producing more than half of the specialist teachers in Rural Studies entering English schools. A breakdown of the student roll for the academic year 1952–3 showed that 65 out of a total of 315 students engaged in courses involving Rural Studies. During the first half of the 1950s, Worcester sought to sharpen its relevance to the needs of the countryside by offering courses specialising in Rural Science for qualified teachers; and at the request of the Ministry of Education, it began providing professional training for agriculture and horticulture graduates. In 1956, responding to the desire of the education authorities in the region for more teachers with expertise in homecraft and cookery, the College set up another course for qualified teachers, covering topics such as bacon curing, milk processing, and fruit and vegetable preservation.

The significance of these courses went beyond the mere techniques, such as sealing bottling jars. They started trends which became a characteristic of Worcester and hold good for the University today. First, they exhibited a readiness to answer the requirements of the local and regional community. Although it is true that, from the 1950s until the late 1980s, the College was answerable to both central government and local authorities, the tradition of response became ingrained, so that the new University actively seeks opportunities to align its teaching with contemporary needs. Second, the provision of courses to those already in the workplace was an acknowledgement that the

STUDENTS AT WORK, 1950S.

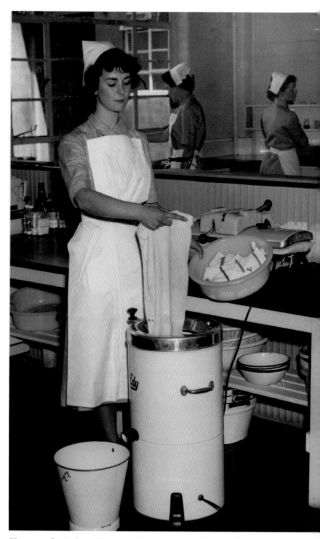

Housecraft student Margaret Robertson loading a spin-dryer in the domestic science kitchen.

Rural crafts being taught by Fred Lambert, far right. The goods produced were sold in a craft shop at the College.

ural husbandry students weighing a beehive.

Rural domestic economy students flower arranging.

Scenes from College open days, 1950s.

College could play a part in what later came to be known as lifelong learning. Worcester would not be an institution just for young people, fresh out of school and looking for one or two degrees; it would be a college where professionals could hone their skills or branch out in new directions, an institution welcoming adults seeking higher education later in life.

Responding to the needs of the general school system proved a more difficult task than accommodating the specific needs of the countryside. Members of the Birmingham Head Teachers' Association, meeting with Peirson and other college principals from around the region during 1954, expressed discontent. They questioned the philosophy of the teacher training college system, the mix of professional training and further education. Teachers were less prepared than in the past and unable to cope with school problems, they complained. All teachers should be able to teach basic subjects. Worcester's external examiners from Birmingham University also had a word on this topic: there was, they reported, 'a lack of distinction' in basic subjects, and they wondered whether the students might be taking them less seriously because they were not a matter of individual choice.

At Worcester staff meetings, Peirson and his staff wrestled with the problem of balance. Staff meetings in 1954 produced two schools of thought: one contending that the personal education of the student is the most valuable way of preparing to teach, and the other favouring a more vocational approach, allowing more time for practical and theoretical work related to classroom activity. Peirson resolved the discussion by deciding that the basic work would be done in the first year, with more concentration on subjects in the second year of the Certificate of Education course. Meanwhile, the College started to offer special education courses for students planning to teach in secondary modern schools, where, in the state system, pupils of average and below average ability tended to go. Teaching practice in the schools in any case had been, and continued to be, an integral part of training, although by 1957 this was becoming increasingly difficult to arrange, with more colleges trying to push their students into a limited number of schools. Even then, the process was somewhat hit-and-miss. An anonymous letter to the *Henwick Herald*, the weekly student news-sheet, bemoaned the disparity between 'modern schools where you plead for two lessons a day' and 'country schools where the one teacher weeps in gratitude at prospects of help for three weeks'.

Teaching practice always produced a flurry of extra activity in the College, leading to competition for books in the library, for example, and sometimes extensive travel, with tutors scurrying round the country to keep check on their charges. It was a break in the comfortable tenor of life in the community at Henwick Grove. All the students lived at the College, which segregated the sexes: men in Block A of the three wartime buildings, and women in Block C. The rooms, Iain Ball remembered, were 'pretty basic', with old furniture,

although there were renewals from time to time. 'You had to walk along miles of corridors to the showers and so on, there was nothing en suite.' But the rooms were warm, 'warmer at college than it was at home', Ball went on. 'It was not a hotel exactly', but it had some of the same features. Cleaners arrived each day to do the rooms; there was clean linen every week; all the meals were provided, plus afternoon tea and an evening snack. Much of the produce came from the College farm and gardens used for Rural Studies training. Dorothy Cattell, who ran the kitchens, was much praised for her catering skills.

But there were niggles. 'More people are made angry by noise in residential blocks than by any other single cause', declared a letter writer in the *Henwick Herald*. Ball agreed. 'The noise was terrible; pipes ran through the rooms from one end of the block to the other, and they carried the sounds. Then there was the clattering in the corridors.' Complaints in the *Henwick Herald* and to the College Committee about daily living were usually trivial, if not frivolous. Could a moving arm 'be attached to ironing boards to prevent the flex from ruffling clothing under treatment?' 'One iron in the west of C block had a broken plug.' There was a demand for a gas lighter in one of the men's utility rooms to stop smokers using pages of the telephone directory as a spill.

Smoking was certainly popular: a 1956 student survey calculated that 45 per cent of the student population smoked, consuming 7,300 cigarettes and 12 ounces of tobacco each week, at a cost of £70, £40 of which was attributed to males, and £30 to females. A cigarette machine, provided free

HM Queen Elizabeth, the Queen Mother, visiting the College's stand at the Three Counties Show, 1958.

E.G. Peirson welcoming The Rt. Hon. Geoffrey Lloyd, Minister of Education, to the College, 1959.

by Players, appeared in 1958, after detailed consideration of how the receipts might be administered.

In the 1950s the College was self-contained, but not exclusive. Few opportunities existed for outside entertainment. The first television did not appear until the Queen's coronation in 1954, when large numbers congregated around a 12-inch set. Cars were rare, so there was little opportunity to dash away from the campus. The College made its own amusement, with sports clubs and the full range of musical, arts and debating societies. Peirson was an aficionado of Gilbert and Sullivan, so there were regular performances of light opera. And the staff participated in all this.

Many staff were resident on the campus, including the Principal – first in B block and then in the house provided for his family and their successors. Grace Peirson remembered the B block flat as 'big and very crude – block walls covered with emulsion paint'. The flat was at one end of the building, leading on to the College grounds, where there was a big apple tree and an area which 'we turned into a lovely garden'. Members of staff practiced their own horticulture, and some even had small numbers of livestock. The Peirson family look back on what they now see as a pampered existence, where Henwick Grove's head gardener 'every week sent up without asking a mass of flowers and vegetables from the gardens'. The staff made up a social community: any special day – Guy Fawkes, Boxing Day, and so on – provoked a gathering of some sort. But the intimacy of the College community could not last. Circumstances on the outside indicated that the College was about to change.

The first part of this change appeared to be principally academic. The government calculated that the school population would decline in the early 1960s. This would provide an opportunity to raise the level of teacher training by extending the Certificate of Education course from two to three years, moving towards a national teaching corps of graduates. The change would take place in 1960,

The College's dairy display at the Three Counties Show, 1958.

the Ministry of Education decreed. This was not a problem for Worcester. When the minister Geoffrey Lloyd visited the College in 1959, he found a ready acceptance of the three-year course and noted that training colleges would become akin to university colleges.

The second change sprang out of a Ministry miscalculation. It decided that its estimate of a decline in the school population was wrong. Rather, it concluded in 1958, the population would increase, with an additional 4,000 places required at training colleges. There would have to be an urgent programme of expansion, based on training colleges where there could be a substantial return for a relatively small outlay. The Treasury's expansion budget for the country was £15m, or £1,500 for every new college place created, as Peirson told the staff. Worcester was one of four colleges in the Birmingham University orbit invited to expand.

Negotiations involving the College, the City of Worcester and the Ministry led to an agreement that Worcester would expand to 550 students in 1962, from the 1958 complement of 350. Such growth made the problem of accommodation acute, even though authority had already been given for a new science block. On the teaching side there would

have to be well-equipped premises for specialist subjects like Home Economics and Rural Studies, as well as Science. The plan accepted by the government involved new teaching, communal and dining accommodation. This would release space for conversion to residential accommodation, so that the number of students living at the College might increase from 300 to 470. Work started on site in April 1960, and by November was already more than two months behind schedule, delayed by bad weather and the departure of construction workers to the more lucrative prospects of motorway building. The new college buildings were not completed until spring 1963, six months after they were required.

Plans for academic and physical expansion brought with it changes inside the College. In line with the regulations of the Institute of Education at Birmingham University, Worcester established its own academic board, responsible for the curriculum, timetable and examinations. The curriculum for the new three-year Certificate of Education had to be settled in detail. It would be based on four sections: the first covered education; the second dealt with subject courses, where a student would study a main subject over three years

Mr J.G. Bell, left, president of The Jersey Cattle Society, shaking hands with E.G. Peirson after presenting the College with a Jersey heifer called Lockyers Scarlet Eileen, 1958.

The College farm changed its dairy herd from Ayrshires, above, to Jerseys.

and a subsidiary subject in the first two years; the third covered professional courses, with one set of topics for potential primary teachers, and another for those going to secondary schools; the fourth section was teaching practice, set at 14 weeks. Administratively, the College looked for refinement.

It was decided that the Union Council, theoretically a meeting of all staff and students, required an executive committee. As Peirson acknowledged, the College was becoming too complicated for him and a Vice Principal to run it. But he did not let go: his interests remained wide enough for him to express a wish that the College farm's dairy herd changed from Ayrshires to Jerseys.

PEIRSON: 1962–78

In 1962, Ned Peirson noted: '350 students went down in July; 550 students came up in October to begin work in new buildings not fully completed'. He had at once moved the training college on to a higher level and brought himself to the peak of his career. Now he faced the start of a period representing strong physical, academic and social development for the College.

The previous years had consolidated the College and the position of Peirson himself, who was a significant figure in Worcester and in the education

Mathematics lecture, 1967.

Joan Russell, left, teaching dance.

profession. He had become a magistrate; he had a diary full of speaking engagements across the region; he was president of the Workers' Educational Association in Worcester; the Ministry of Education brought him on to a working party looking at ways of increasing the number of specialist mathematics teachers; he was a senior member of the Association of Teachers in Colleges and Departments of Education; and he was on the sponsoring committee for the proposed university college of Gloucestershire. Peirson's relations with Worcester City Council's education authorities, his employer, were close and amiable – so amiable that one education officer is permanently remembered on the campus through the Chandler building.

Inside the College, he was the despot who listened. Doreen Milton, his secretary at one stage, found 'he was a person you could talk to. He was considerate, and if a piece of work had figures I automatically checked them and he never made a fuss about corrections. He had such friendliness. He made a point of getting to know every student by name.' Indeed, as Philip Hytch, who arrived at the College as a lecturer in 1960, explained, he only stopped interviewing potential students late in his career. Although Peirson won respect as a manager, his style remained informal. 'When we had a senior common room', Hytch recollected, 'he was always there at coffee and tea times. He never sat down, he would stand there with his cup and saucer held close to his chin and chat with the people who came to him. That was how he did his business.' Iain Ball, one of the students Peirson interviewed, found that he would always give people the benefit of the doubt: 'he was avuncular, patriarchal – all-

embracing'. So all-embracing, in fact, that doctors told him his style of running the College was not sensible and he should learn to interact with fewer people. By all accounts, he did try to do this, but, said Grace Peirson, 'he didn't want to take holidays. He'd come home at the end of the day – he didn't want to talk – he just sat in a comfortable chair.'

For all that, Peirson managed to surround himself with staff who blossomed at Worcester and whose influence spread far beyond. Indeed, there was a gathering of educational talent across a range of disciplines which few other colleges could match, with specialists in Rural Studies making their mark early on. Harold Watkins Shaw, whose edition of Handel's *Messiah* was published in 1959 and remains in use, was a musician of merit. Ethel Dodge and Muriel Stone were experts in primary and infant education. Joan Russell, a great favourite of Peirson, was a dance teacher of international renown. Fred Grice became a poet, author of children's stories, and a local broadcaster and critic. Cyril Hope and, later, Irene Campbell made signal contributions to mathematical education through the Midlands Mathematical Experiment, which was based at Worcester. After the Nuffield Foundation made £250,000 available in 1962, for a long-term programme to develop new techniques of science and mathematics teaching, Ted Wenham, a physicist of note, became an organiser of the Ordinary Level physics project, and Jon Ogborn later became responsible for the Advanced Level physics project (the 'Nuffield' approach followed by David Green, as a schoolboy, later to become the first Vice Chancellor of the University of Worcester).

Grace Peirson cannot remember exactly when her husband started talking of the teachers training college becoming a university, but it began to figure in domestic conversation during the early 1960s. She knew that he wanted the status of teachers to be lifted, and that he chafed at the salary difference between those trained in the colleges and those graduating from universities. Clearly Worcester was too small in 1962 for university status to be a realistic option, but scarcely had the October intake settled down than Peirson was planning further expansion. He told the College governors in June 1963 that the Ministry of

NEW BUILDINGS, OPENED OFFICIALLY IN 1964.

Communal areas for study and socialising.

The main entrance.

Student study areas/common room.

The new agriculture lecture theatre.

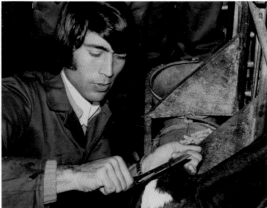

Foreign agricultural students came to the College from all over the world. During the 1970s the College had a contract to train Afghan farmers.

Education had agreed to include Worcester in the list of colleges selected for enlargement, but thought that the target should be around 900 students, if no more than one-third of them lived in lodgings. This was 120 fewer than Peirson had hoped for. But then came the Robbins report, which would change the face of British tertiary education.

The Robbins Committee, officially the Committee on Higher Education, appointed in 1961, called for massive expansion in higher education over the next 17 years, with six new universities and ten existing institutions transformed into universities. Training colleges, which had 55,000 students nationally, should accommodate 146,000 by 1980–1. Fortuitously, Harold Wilson, who had made a clarion call for a revolution in education, promised a 'tremendous building programme of new universities' in his first speech to the Labour Party conference as leader. There was, in short, a

swell of opinion in favour of change. It provided just the impetus Peirson needed and allowed him to articulate his vision of an optimistic future: 'A University of Worcester about 1980 is a realistic prospect and I firmly believe that this should be the ambition to guide our progress from now on.'

The path of progress towards this goal would not be an easy one. The City of Worcester seemed slower on the uptake than Peirson himself. There was reluctance in the Education Department to lend concrete support, reported the *Worcester Evening News*. Peirson recognised there would be competition: he told the newspaper that similar colleges in the region – Gloucester, Kidderminster, Wolverhampton – would be looking in the same direction. He was right. Both Gloucester and Wolverhampton became universities before Worcester. Peirson's assessment that university status was feasible proved correct, but his prediction was 25 years premature.

He understood that Worcester's position would gain strength the larger it became. Robbins had said that 2,000 students was a minimum for a putative university; if a college was to expand to acquire that status, it would be exceptional to have fewer than 750 students. The authorised increase in student numbers to more than 900 would clearly be important for laying the base of Worcester's claim. But more immediate issues demanded attention.

The post-war bulge in the birth rate left the Department of Education and Science (DES), as the Ministry had become, grappling with teacher shortages. In 1965 it asked colleges to increase their student intake by 20 per cent. Two years later it returned to the same theme, requesting that colleges put forward proposals for further enlargement, making it clear that only a minority would be selected. Worcester came back with a scheme to raise its student roll to 1,660 by 1974–5. This proved too much for the DES, which in 1969 accepted a student target figure of 1,225.

The running negotiation over numbers accompanied parallel negotiation over the physical facilities. Peirson would have liked major land purchases and extensive new building. But the DES wanted expansion at minimum cost; this it could achieve in part by having a growing proportion of students living outside the College, thus removing the need for more residential blocks, and it sought fuller use of existing teaching facilities. So, for Worcester, physical expansion involved just a 60-bed block for women, a building to act as a base for students coming from outside the area, and some extra teaching accommodation. The days of the cosy residential community had come to an end.

Academic change went alongside the growth of the College. Retrospectively, it is clear that a chain of

events began in the late 1960s which would lead, eventually, to the academic independence of the institution as a university. Worcester had been uneasy about its position as a constituent college, academically under the wing of Birmingham University's Institute of Education. The breach finally came over the conditions for running the four-year Bachelor of Education (BEd) course, an innovation advocated by the Robbins committee.

For Robbins, academic development went hand in hand with the expansion of numbers in the teacher training system. The BEd would both raise the educational standard of students in the system and lift their status by the grant of a degree, a

Teacher training at Henwick Grove Primary School, 1967.

higher qualification than a certificate. The extra year would come on top of the three-year work for a Certificate of Education, by offering study of a particular subject. For Peirson and Worcester, this was not a problem. But Worcester – renamed the Worcester College of Education in September 1965 – wanted to advance in one way and Birmingham in another.

Birmingham wanted to restrict the subjects offered in the fourth year to those which it taught itself. Worcester wanted no limitation on subjects, because the Birmingham approach would automatically rule out 30 per cent of the Worcester intake by not embracing areas like Rural Studies, Domestic Science and Dance. Worcester was not happy with the way in which discussion about the syllabus and examinations excluded some of the colleges in the Birmingham Institute of Education constituency. It felt that Birmingham was taking an unnecessarily rigid view of entry requirements for the fourth year, and would not accept the proposal that all the teaching should take place in Birmingham.

When it became clear that these issues would probably remain unresolved, Peirson received the approval of the College governors for talks with other institutions about the validation of Worcester courses. There was a brief dalliance with the University of Warwick, but a natural home was just around the corner, at the Council for National Academic Awards (CNAA).

At the CNAA, Worcester would meet no restrictions on subjects; it would be able to produce its own syllabuses for CNAA approval; it would take responsibility for teaching; and it would conduct its own examinations, in association with CNAA-approved external examiners. The College would be taking significant steps towards an independence impossible under the wing of

Student using overhead projector in Educational Technology Centre, 1974.

Early computing.

Weighing a gerbil in a biology lecture, 1967.

Local school children on a visit to the College farm.

...hion show by third-year students in the ...dlecraft Department, 1970.

The Peirson Library opened in 1973.

Birmingham University.

But it took some years to bring about. Talks took place with the CNAA, and CNAA officials visited the College in 1966 and assured themselves that the general requirements for providing courses leading to degrees were being met. But then the fields lay fallow. A CNAA panel made another visit in 1969, but only in 1973 and 1974 did the College prepare and make detailed submissions, which led to the CNAA sending a team of 35 to scrutinise every aspect of the College's business. Satisfied, the CNAA prepared to award its degrees to Worcester students for six years, starting with those admitted in September 1975. But it laid down some conditions. The college library needed 20 per cent more books; links between the different subjects studied should be explored; there should be 15 weeks of school experience; and subject options needed to be reviewed every year, given the uncertainty at that point about the number of students going into teacher training.

In the 11 years between the Robbins report, with the heady expectations it aroused, and the alliance between Worcester and the CNAA, the atmosphere changed, as did demands on the colleges. There had been talk in official education circles of restricting the role of the teachers training colleges to preparing students solely for primary school teaching, and concentrating on bringing in more female students, but all this had petered out. For the 1960s generally, expansion was the keyword and the Wilson Government – economic woes notwithstanding – funded the Robbins recommendations. Significant among these was the Open University, which opened an outpost on the College campus in 1970. Towards the end of the decade, the expansion machine began to splutter. Worcester governors started to express concern at a DES idea that an increase in student numbers taking the BEd course should be offset by reductions in other courses.

By the time Margaret Thatcher, the Education Secretary climbing the political ranks, introduced her White Paper in 1973, Worcester and other colleges faced the uncomfortable situation of a drop in demand for teachers. They would have to find ways of compensating for the probable fall in student numbers, or they might go under. The White Paper noted that many colleges were small and inconveniently located, but others could branch out and grow. 'Some colleges, either singly or jointly, should develop... into major institutions of higher education, concentrating on the arts and human sciences, with particular reference to their application in training and other professions.' Here, for Peirson, was the opportunity to counter the threat. He took it. He started on 'a steeplechase', as John Nixon, then a young lecturer in the early

The Peirson Library today.

stages of a Worcester career, described it. 'Many colleges fell down. The core of many institutions was weaker than Worcester's. Some amalgamated and some closed, like Hereford and Bromsgrove.' Philip Hytch commented, 'They faded away, these smaller colleges, because they didn't pursue a rigorous enough policy in the courses they were teaching'. Worcester must innovate to survive, said Peirson in a 1974 speech.

The College's academic board was quick to devise (and the governors equally quick to sanction) a plan for a range of courses. The three-year Certificate of Education would be phased out and replaced by three and four-year BEd courses, up to honour level, for students with two advanced level passes in the General Certificate of Education; there would be a three-year general degree course for students not wishing to be teachers; there would

be a two-year course for the Diploma of Higher Education (DipHE), which could be the base for a Bachelor of Arts (BA) degree course; and the College would continue its courses for those already professionally qualified. In conclusion, the academic board declared, 'the College should develop into a major institution of higher education [in line with the White Paper]... with all award-bearing courses validated by CNAA'. The DES accepted all this, although it made clear that it would not accept heavy capital expenditure plans.

That acceptance, coupled with agreement from the CNAA to validate degrees from Worcester – the first college of education for which it acted in this way – swung the College out of a gentle educational backwater and into the mainstream of British higher education. Indeed, from September 1976, even the title changed again – this time to

Alumnae reminiscing.

Then and now: rugby team, 1950 and reunited in 2005.

Worcester College of Higher Education. Peirson had ensured the College's survival and mapped a future. He may not have made a university, but he had taken useful steps towards it and had reached the pinnacle of his career.

For all the achievements, Peirson had to handle difficult years as he approached retirement. In some respects, the College had grown and changed too fast for its organisation and habits of working. Pressures accumulated outside and circumstances beyond his control botched the succession.

A visiting party from the CNAA pinpointed the internal problems. The College had too many departments – 16 in all – and the academic structure had become too varied: education studies had 34 members of staff, but handicrafts only 2. Lines of communication in the College had become blurred. There was an impression, the CNAA reported, that the academic board 'had not yet fully entered into its responsibilities as the College's major decision-making and policy-making body'. What is more, the CNAA visitors 'felt that the College as a whole was still thinking in terms of a college of education in which the important decisions were left to the Principal and his heads of department'. The CNAA saw it as axiomatic that if a college offered degrees it should have an appreciable research programme, but this was not the case at Worcester. It was worried too that necessary increases in technical and clerical staff had not been implemented.

Staff increases depended at least in part on the new Hereford and Worcester County Council, into

E.G. Peirson's retirement procession, 1978.

whose charge the College had been placed as part of a broader reorganisation of local government. But the County Council, according to the CNAA, had 'not yet fully appreciated difficulties faced by the College in coming to terms with its new role'. Peirson then faced dealing with new masters as well as having to superintend the major administrative changes which followed from the change in the status of the College.

Gone were the days when Peirson could comfortably arrange affairs with the education authorities of the City of Worcester. Instead there were niggles with the County Council over relatively small financial matters, like raising the rents of College houses without telling the College. In fact, there was a running argument, lasting four years, about the replacement of the building where the College kept its farm animals. The County Council, of course, saw the College not as a unique institution, but rather as part of the county bureaucracy, and expected it to bear its share of the financial worries caused by rampant inflation in the mid 1970s: hence the 1975 demand for a five per cent cut in costs. The effects of this were felt keenly because, as Peirson said, 'it bears most heavily on budgets which lie within the control of the college', leading to continued postponement of maintenance work.

At the end of 1976, the College Governors appointed Walter James, a senior academic at the Open University, as Peirson's successor. Peirson himself had prepared for retirement and he was

ready for it, Grace Peirson remembered, but in May 1977, James withdrew, evidently dissatisfied with the accommodation arrangements (a Principal's house had been built in the early 1960s). The governors asked Peirson to hold the fort. 'It shouldn't have happened. It was a struggle. He drove himself to work. He lived for the College', Grace said. Within 18 months of retiring at the end of the 1978 spring term, Ned Peirson succumbed to leukemia and passed away in 1980.

Next page: The main entrance.

Chapter Four

No end, but All an Upward Path to Climb

The second attempt to find a successor to Ned Peirson produced 219 enquiries and 63 applications. The governors chose David Shadbolt, Principal of the Northumberland College of Higher Education, to start in the summer term of 1978, just in time to inherit one of the last of Peirson's internal measures. He arrived as Worcester brought into play a new system of organisation, based around three schools – Education and Teaching Studies, Arts, and Sciences – with divisions concerned with individual subjects. On top of the schools, two faculty boards – one for the education side, the other for arts and sciences – administered and controlled studies. The academic board, relieved of responsibilities for the detail of scholarship, concentrated on planning and resources, research and staff development, student services and welfare.

Shadbolt did not tamper with this arrangement. Three months after his arrival, he confided to the governors that he had taken over 'a College in good heart'. At the end of his first year, according to notes he made for a governors' meeting, he wrote: 'I have inherited good capital which I must use wisely. My colleagues, both academic and non-academic are remarkable by any standards.' Inevitably, the way in which he used the capital and worked with colleagues proved different from Peirson's style.

Opposite: Woodcut from College magazine, 1947.

Experiments in plant breeding, 1978.

By all accounts, Shadbolt, more introverted than his predecessor, had a detached, even clinical, approach, which left little opportunity for extensive contact with staff and students. He was a shy man, 'angular socially', as one friend put it, a man who did not suffer fools gladly, and who would ride over dissidents. 'Really he could only relax with those whom he trusted', recalled Helen Ball, an alumna of the College and governor during the Shadbolt years. One former member of staff contrasted two aspects of Shadbolt. On the one hand, there was the back-room executive whose administration was clean, who was good on paper. Indeed, the College papers show a man with a clear, methodical mind, assured in both defining policy and capturing detail. On the other hand, there was the complaint: 'We never saw him and he never saw us. He conducted academic board meetings with his eyes closed. I mean that literally.'

This appearance of remoteness has tended to overshadow Shadbolt's reputation and to push into the background his achievement, guiding the College through the harshest period of its existence. Pressures had begun to build in Peirson's last years, but, even allowing for the problems of taking the College in new directions, Peirson had enjoyed expansion and the prospect of growth. Hines, of course, had established the College and set its early tone. But for Shadbolt there were no certainties. His tenure coincided with the Thatcher and Major Governments; as they bore down on government spending and attacked the traditional characteristics of higher education, Shadbolt and Worcester were caught in the backwash. Shadbolt then had to deal with financial cuts, which damaged both the physical and the academic structure of the College; new forms of central control; and, finally, incorporation, which involved responsibility without full control.

In an atmosphere of financial stringency, Shadbolt quickly realised that expectations of growth would be slower than Peirson had envisaged – gradual rather than explosive. Problems of accommodation 'are likely to be acute before any new buildings arise'. Major building plans would not be considered until 1980, which meant they would not be included in any programmes until 1982–3 at the earliest, he told the governors during 1979. Maintenance work had been delayed; the backlog had been growing for four or five years, particularly where teaching accommodation was concerned.

The first half of Shadbolt's tenure proved very uncomfortable. In fact, it was so unsettling that in July 1982 he confessed to the governors: 'This year has been one of the most traumatic the College has ever experienced; as a matter of record I view it as one of the worst of my professional life.' The effects of contraction accumulated.

The 1978–9 College budget had been approved by the county at a lower level than had been recommended. The 1979–80 budget lowered the provision for care of buildings and grounds. The County Council education committee demanded a 2.5 per cent reduction in the base budget for 1980–1, when in more normal circumstances, taking into account inflation, there should have been a rise of 15.9 per cent on that approved for the

Sculpting in the art studio.

previous year. Hardly had this been absorbed than the County Council wanted a deeper cut still, of 0.5 per cent over and above the 2.5 per cent. And so it went on: 1981–2, 1982–3, 1984–5. In fact, the College found itself caught in a vice, with the County Council applying pressure on one side and central government on the other. The greatest part of the College's funding came from the Advanced Further Education Pool, established in part by payments from local authorities. But a lid was placed on these funds for 1980–1: there would be a finite sum to share between all the colleges. The allocations would be based on 50 per cent of the actual expenditure in 1978–9, and the remaining 50 per cent on the forecasts for 1980–1. Budgeting, declared some of Shadbolt's notes from 1983, was 'a nightmare'.

The County Council had its own problems. Like other local authorities, it was a butt of the Thatcher Government's efforts to reduce public expenditure. Like the government itself, the County Council tried to increase its resources by selling assets which it decided were no longer a public requirement. This had become fashionable by 1983, as the government moved into its programme of selling state corporations, and the pace of housing sales to council tenants quickened. So Hereford and Worcester looked to find property assets which could be sold, initiating the Worcester property study to examine its holdings in the city. That included the Worcester College of Higher Education.

The property study set off a chain of events recalled with bitterness well into the 21st century. Early in the 1980s, County Council officers concluded that Henwick House, used, among other things, for practical studies in Home Economics and Rural Studies, was surplus to college requirements. At different times, they jumped on ideas that the House would be suitable as lodgings for circuit

An experiment in the Science Department, 1978.

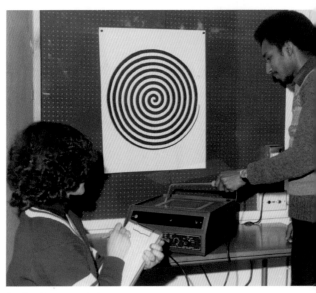

Performing a psychology test.

The Peirson Library, 1978.

A music group.

Students stage a dance performance.

court judges and for use by Worcester Technical College; they made some 30 visits to the property without contacting the College, so that Shadbolt and the governors remained ignorant of the proposals (eventually stillborn) until autumn 1981. The crucial event, though, was the March 1983 agreement between the College governors and the County Council. This set out a scheme for development, which acknowledged that the residential areas (the old wartime buildings) were sub-standard, that teaching accommodation needed to be supplemented and that, although there was sufficient communal accommodation, it was of poor quality.

The essence of the deal involved a programme of land sales running into 1987–8, the proceeds of which could be directed towards new buildings. For the governors, the attraction was pump-priming at a time when there seemed to be no other source of cash. The property study itself stated that, 'Any sales proceeds generated by the College should be reinvested in the campus in order to improve the overall quality of accommodation.' The governors accepted the trade-off, 'subject to funds being made available to provide the first phase of the development plan', although this was not without misgivings: the sales might prejudice later developments; no technique other than self-contained financing of development appears to have been explored; and the mid 1980s was not the best time to be putting land on the market. The sales, involving parcels of land around the periphery of the College property, including Henwick House and its immediate surroundings, duly began. The immediate return to the College was a new residential block, and at one stage the County Council ran a financial deficit on the development plan: it had received £1.5m but spent £1m more.

But the financial environment changed. By 1987–8, a nationwide property boom was under way. In addition, the County Council knew that in 1989 the College would pass out of its control. The last parcel of land, adjacent to the College's main entrance and close to the library, realised £3.5m, leaving the property study plans with a surplus of £3m, a sum roughly equivalent to the cost of Worcester's staff for an entire year. 'The governors wished to know whether the College would benefit from this windfall profit on the sale of its land. It was agreed that the Principal would approach the County Council on this matter and the governors declared their full support from this action', noted the minutes of a meeting in June 1988. The property study declaration of 1983 appears to have been forgotten.

Negotiations over the next five months led to agreement by the County Council for a £750,000 programme of refurbishments on the campus. The County Council kept the balance of £2.75m, and ever since has been the target of criticism, accused, in the phrase made famous by Harold Macmillan in the House of Lords, of selling the family silver. Philip Hytch, the College lecturer who became a city councillor and eventually Mayor of Worcester, accused the County Council of 'monstrous behaviour', reported the *Worcester Evening News*. Other councillors called it 'cavalier', 'appaling',

'asset stripping'. All that said, the County Council acted completely within its rights, holding to the belief that, as part of the council apparatus, the College had to make a contribution to its finances.

One factor which made the land sales easier was the decision of the College to abandon Rural Studies as an economy measure. This helped to release some of the property at and around Henwick House, making it easier to sell as a private residence or residences. This is just one example of the way in which financial pressures gnawed at the academic life of the College during the 1980s.

Shadbolt's first year concentrated, as he put it, on 'academic consolidation', with an active concern about studies for those not planning to enter teaching, aware that growth would tend to arise from the approval and validation by the CNAA of

The Digital Arts Centre, opened in 2001, houses multimedia computers, scanners and printers. The DAC also has sound and video recording and editing equipment in specialist studios and a big digitally enhanced performance and video recording space.

Outdoor recreation.

new courses and programmes. But this would not be as simple as it appeared at first sight. 'A major constraint on making planned development is the lack of external policy and planning which frustrates the capacity of the College to exploit the resources in difficult circumstances', said Shadbolt's review of 1980. Further, it was not clear how the 'difficult circumstances' might affect a college which had a tendency for its courses and programmes to share both human and physical facilities. 'If the budget strategy leads, for example, to a reduction of teaching staff establishment, there is the real problem of toppling the whole structure, since all parts interlock.'

The first cuts, affecting the non-academic staff, prompted the CNAA to warn, in 1981, that reductions to support services had reached such a level that any further cuts would represent a threat to academic standards. The following year, reductions spread inexorably to the academic staff: the schools of arts and sciences merged and Shadbolt sought to lose 15 posts, five from education and teaching studies, two from arts, six from sciences and two from academic administration. It was at this point that the Rural Studies division closed. Another nine academic staff went in 1983: two by resignation who were not replaced, and seven through voluntary early retirement.

Between 1981 and 1983, the academic staff was reduced by 20 per cent, to 98. Nevertheless, noted a 1983 review of the College's academic development, 'the College is larger now in student numbers (at 1300) than it has ever been; it is teaching to higher standards than ever before; the curriculum has a wider range and more diverse modes of attendance than ever before'. Certainly, the era of exclusive teacher training had come to an end; the College had nearly 500 students following BA, BSc and DipHE courses in programmes under the label of general higher education. Furthermore, the College had moved away from concentrating purely on students straight from school; the number of mature and part-time students had risen steadily as the College tried to play a greater role in the regional economy.

Although the College dealt with continuing uncertainty about the intentions of central government for the number of teachers required and the role of Worcester in providing them, it managed to forge a view of its own future. The academic board 'sustains a view of an institution with a widely diversified curriculum in breadth and depth offering national courses more specifically tailored for its region. The Board's long term view is of a significant institution limited in scope by realistic criteria but not limited in quality or responsibility – a country polytechnic.' Peirson's early vision had not been blurred, for the academic

The University of Worcester offers a variety of courses designed for educational support workers, including teaching assistants.

board's diagnosis of Worcester's role could be seen as a stepping stone to university status.

Against the background of shifting plans and aspirations, the CNAA had been a constant element, underpinning the academic status of the College. Its institutional review of 1986 accepted that Worcester 'should continue in approval as a suitable environment for the conduct of courses leading to the Council's awards'. Yet its report implied that the activities of the College had become thinly spread, as it returned to the same theme which had been a source of concern during Peirson's day: it is 'not clear whether the College would be able to continue meeting the rising expectations of academic staff and students from its support staffing'. The next step for the College, in the growing maturity of its operations, would be for it to go beyond having its degrees validated by the CNAA to having the CNAA accredit the College itself – that is, the College would be granted authority by the CNAA both to run and to examine its courses. The CNAA would step back, in effect, to the role of benevolent, supervising uncle. But the CNAA did not think that Worcester could sustain such autonomy: it is 'not clear whether the College's central administration would be able to

provide the support for the operation of an institutional agreement, should a full delegated authority agreement be sought'. This was a check to the College's development, but, as events would prove, it did not much matter for the long run.

—

The world of higher education changed in 1987, with the publication of the government's White Paper, Meeting the Challenge, and the consequent Education Reform Act of 1988, and Worcester changed within it.

Like 24 polytechnics and 26 other higher education colleges, Worcester would become a corporation with independent status, freed from local authority control. Shadbolt would now report only to the governors, the majority of whom would have to come from the private sector, reflecting the government's policy of moving the whole of the higher education sector closer to business. It would no longer receive grants; instead, a system of annual contracts went into place, placing the College in a direct relationship with the Polytechnics and Colleges Funding Council (PCFC), and later with Higher Education Funding Council for England (HEFCE). Through the PCFC, the DES would approve courses and set the targets for teacher training. Worcester would have to compete for what it wanted. All of this combined to place the College and those who ran it in uncharted waters, demanding new skills and changed habits.

First reactions in Worcester were cautious at best. The County Council was against the provisions of the Act, for obvious reasons. The academic board doubted the practicality of one-year contracts. Such doubts carried little weight. Higher Education Corporations were established constitutionally in November 1988, and vesting day for the new bodies was set for April 1989. But the preparations started well before that. The first chairman of the governors, provisionally chairman of the formation committee, was Raymond George, formerly managing director of Royal Worcester, the china group. It was a measure of the shock to the College's system that, in spring 1988, George wrote to Shadbolt, setting out the steps that would need to be taken towards the creation of a business plan. Writing business plans had not been necessary when a local authority controlled the money.

Shadbolt had paid the price of local authority control in the form of a perpetual tussle over even small expenditure. With incorporation he would at least be spared arguments over spending on items like the installation of hand basins in bedrooms. Harassed in 1985 over a long series of small queries about budget variations, he was driven to complain to the county education officer, 'In general it must be said that I am an academic administrator, not an accountant, trying to balance the conflicting demands of central and local authorities to sustain the academic and financial credibility of the college in a professional manner.' With the onset of incorporation, the academic administrator found himself faced with an organisational maelstrom, the appearance of independence thrust upon him.

1984 field trip.

Next page: Springtime on the campus.

Chapter Five

ALL IS WILD WITH CHANGE

Fresh duties and responsibilities fell on the College at incorporation. A new governing body dominated by the private sector, people who were not necessarily familiar with the running of academic institutions, and new articles of governance had to bed down. For the first time, David Shadbolt and the College authorities had to negotiate directly with the trade unions; they had to come to terms with independent financial management, while the central government demanded indicators of academic performance to help settle the new funding arrangements through the PCFC (and later the HEFCE); they also had to contend with making their own insurance arrangements. Simultaneously, they were seeking to give the College a competitive academic edge.

The shock of change was felt most keenly with the management of funds. Internally, Shadbolt had always kept a tight rein on the budget, but because the College had been part of the County Council, it did not have a finance system; the County Council even took care of the payroll. Pat Finch came from the County Council to be the first Director of Finance. 'The appointment seemed almost an afterthought', she remembered. 'The College had chosen a finance system but it had no qualified accountant. I had five or six staff but none were qualified. So we had to start from scratch.' To begin with, all the money was managed centrally; delegation, giving senior academic staff a measure

The Hot-spots band by T. Yeo from the College magazine, 1954.

of control over their own budgets, did not come until the 1990s.

Externally, the College had to compete for funds as it entered into competitive tendering. In January 1990, it won its first competitive tender since incorporation, when it obtained a two-year commitment to provide nursing training at the Hereford and Worcester School of Nursing. But with the PCFC it pitched its bids too high for funding attached to student numbers and faced a loss of central funding of £145,000. It was a salutary lesson and the search for cuts in overheads led to six voluntary redundancies of academic staff. It also exposed the weaknesses of the College at that time, as Shadbolt laid out starkly in a memorandum placed on staff notice boards:

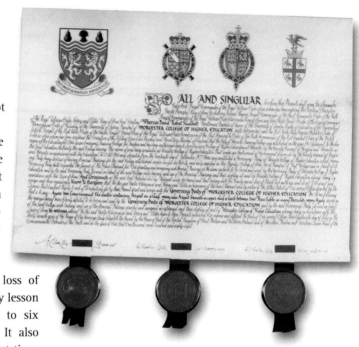

College Letters Patent and Grant of Arms, 1988.

> The tendering system did permit claims of 'quality' to be made. The criteria of 'quality' were judged PCFC programme area by PCFC programme area: in our case science, computing, economics, humanities, performing arts and education. We have no single subject honours degrees outside education; no specialist courses outside education identifying us as market leaders. We have no externally funded research in these areas, nor in education. In education, our roll (on entry and all years) has not made target for some years. Our student population is predominantly white, 18 years old with two 'A' levels.

Disappointments notwithstanding, academic developments came in a rush during the years immediately after incorporation and before Shadbolt's retirement in the summer of 1992. The College introduced new courses in social biology, psychology, environmental management, organisational studies, leisure management and European studies. It also started a DipHE in nursing studies. In the dying months of the CNAA (the government having decided to wind it up), the College tried, but failed, to gain the accreditation which the CNAA had been so chary about during the 1980s. This led Shadbolt to Coventry University, which agreed to validate Worcester degrees from 1994. Talks began about merging the School of Nursing with the College. For Shadbolt, this was a significant move, because the government's attempts to break up the traditional patterns of teacher training, in 1991, led it to toy with the idea of taking some training out of colleges and putting it into schools. Any move

The main entrance in the autumn.

on those lines would cut into the Worcester student roll, and hence into its central funding. Bringing in the School of Nursing, if nothing else, would keep up the College numbers.

Shadbolt's legacy at Worcester was considerable. His activities formed an essential base for what would come later, not least on the financial side. Pat Finch recalled how he always kept within the College budget, and how he declared his ambition to leave the College with a financial surplus. He kept to his word. In the 1991–2 fiscal year, the surplus was £663,535, bringing the retained surplus to £1.097m, and prompting KPMG Peat Marwick, the College auditors, to comment on 'a strong financial position for the College'. Shadbolt made future expansion possible. More than that, his prudence in a hostile environment kept the College alive during a period when so many colleges closed that the government had to create a special staff redundancy package.

With incorporation, he helped to bed in a fresh organisation, so that his successors could concentrate on their visions of development. He had weaned the College from dependence to independence. By the time he retired, the College had become accustomed to taking its own decisions, to making its own way in a more competitive world.

Shadbolt had begun to take the College into the community. Evidently he had little time for local politicians, and he kept dealings with the local press to a minimum, but that did not prevent a slightly raised profile for the College in the town and across the region. Shadbolt initiated the graduation ceremonies in Worcester Cathedral; he had the

Dorma Urwin, Principal, 1992–2002, embraced all aspects of college life.

College join the Chamber of Commerce; and he brought an Education Industry Centre and a Regional Resources Centre to the College. He was also alert to the possibilities of bringing in students from outside the College's recruiting base in the county. John Nixon, responsible for the Postgraduate Certificate of Education courses during the 1980s, recalled how Shadbolt found a market in Ireland, causing uproar in the Republic and Northern Ireland universities; he was so successful that Irish students formed eight per cent of the student roll in 1990. At the same time, Shadbolt was conscientious in maintaining ties with alumni. 'He couldn't be faulted', Helen Ball remembered. 'He put himself about, talked at dinners and so on. He socialised. He always delivered what the Old Students Association asked for.' Again, there was a base for his successor to build on.

The search for a successor began in 1991. According to those who took part in the process, there was one candidate who stood out: Dorma Urwin. 'She knocked the spots off the other candidates, the grey suits. She had vision, a different feel.' She came with credit for playing a major part in the transformation of the once troubled Polytechnic of North London.

Once in position, Urwin acknowledged the past and looked immediately to the future. At a governors' meeting towards the end of 1992, Raymond George 'welcomed the smooth transition from Dr Shadbolt as Principal to Ms Urwin as Principal'. Urwin herself made clear her appreciation of Shadbolt, but wasted no time in articulating the prospect of a very different Worcester College.

Doing this outside the College was not Shadbolt's style, but one of Urwin's first actions was to give the College a public face, and to offer the people of Hereford and Worcester an aspiration: it is 'a great shame the College is not more visible within the city and county... There is no sense of civic pride in this major intellectual resource. It has not been properly marketed and exploited', she told the *Worcester Evening News*. The aspiration was a return to the ambition of Ned Peirson: 'University status is our objective.' Expansion would be an immediate aim, with an effort to double the number of students, both full-time and part-time. An expanding college, as she put it wryly in reference to the recession then gripping the UK, is 'one of the few growth industries at the moment'.

She wasted no time in setting to work. 'She was so enthusiastic, prepared to consider everything. She was an extrovert. And she realised that if the College expanded it would be less vulnerable to a takeover or merger', Pat Finch remembered. She eased out of position senior staff members whom she considered unsuitable, for whatever reason. She strengthened the management team, the executive group made up of directors of the main College functions, but tried to push authority down the hierarchy and break the hold of the deans on finance for academic purposes, by delegating more authority to departments. Later she created a wider forum which gave a louder voice to the academic departments, the Principal's management advisory group. But as Urwin settled into her position, she became increasingly reliant on an inner group. Three men were crucial: Dick Bryant, the Vice Principal, who, fortuitously, had been a colleague at the Polytechnic of North London; Martin Doughty, who was responsible for the introduction of the undergraduate modular system, a vital tool of the expansion policy; and Rod Coveney, the registrar and clerk to the board, who had started at Worcester in 1966 as a physical education lecturer, before proving to be a skilled administrator. When Coveney retired, John Ryan followed in the same role, bringing to the running of the College and the University a national reputation as an academic administrator.

The climate for expansion in the early 1990s proved benign. In a move evoking memories of the 1960s Robbins report, in 1991, the government published the White Paper, Higher Education: A New Framework. This made a commitment to provide college and university places for one-third of school leavers and people in early maturity by the year 2000. Subsequently, the HEFCE published

Cycling on campus.

figures showing 67 per cent growth in student numbers between 1988–9 and 1993–4, before a levelling-off later in the decade. To some extent, Worcester could ride on the back of that trend, but to achieve the ambition of creating a university, as Urwin had set out, the College needed a higher profile, or, to put it another way, a stronger competitive position in the academic world.

Work needed to continue on making College courses of a high quality (HEFCE assessors rapped the College's wrist during the mid 1990s over its music course) and of relevant diversity. The College had a strong foundation for the latter in the variety of expertise it had accumulated in earlier years to cater for the subject needs of teachers. At the same time, the College needed to augment its research in order to create an environment attractive to graduates. Academic strength would be the basis for attracting not only graduates, but also an undergraduate population from varied backgrounds, from the region, from around the UK and from abroad. This population needed facilities in which to live, work and play, and they could not be provided unless the College had a solid financial footing. All the elements of expansion linked together: scholarship, recruitment, building. The high energy devoted to each is the story of the Urwin years.

The first students for the undergraduate modular scheme (UMS) entered the College in September 1994. This was the first of two salient academic developments in the early years of Urwin's tenure. Worcester had been offering a BA in Combined Studies: the UMS took that as a starting point and made the combined studies approach more flexible. Instead of two or three subjects studied at length, the UMS provided for a greater range of subjects that a student could take towards a degree – more subjects, less time on each.

Rehearsing for Much Ado About Nothing, *1994.*

This was, as Dick Bryant recollected, 'a bold exercise'; at the time, UMS was not widespread among British institutions and there was no guarantee that it would attract students in the numbers the College hoped. But it did 'allow development of part time courses which could piggy-back on full time courses, it allowed flexible pathways to a degree and it allowed the curriculum to adjust quickly to changes in demand'. Inside the College there was some distrust. 'Staff didn't like the philosophy of bite-sized chunks of education, examined at the end of the module. But gradually the reservations faded', Bryant noted, and UMS eventually became the centrepiece of the College's undergraduate curriculum. 'Had it gone sour, it would have prejudiced our intake and, more crucially, the vision', Rod Coveney observed.

The second salient development was the completion of negotiations and the incorporation of the Hereford and Worcester School of Nursing into

Sports student.

At work on a river studies field trip in Slovenia.

Geography lecturer, Dr Derek McDougall,
using the latest presentation equipment.

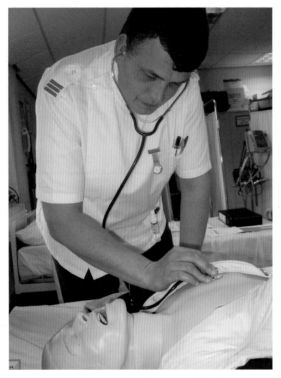

Nursing student at work on the innovative 'Sim Man'.

Worcester. The effect was to open up the new field of Health Studies in the College's academic offering, as tuition could branch out from nursing and midwifery into the wider provision of health professional training. Health studies re-emphasized the vocational quality of extensive sections of college activity, and provided a link to Shadbolt, whose notes for a July 1979 meeting of governors declared 'an increased interest in vocational activities and in widened education to prepare young people for the future'.

At the same time, the merger gave a stimulus to Urwin's academic reorganisation at Worcester. She inherited two schools: Arts and Sciences with 55 staff, and Education with 41. In the revised 1993–7 strategic plan – the first for the College and

compulsory under HEFCE funding arrangements – Urwin doubled the number of schools, both to flatten the management of the College and to sharpen the 'academic and professional focus'. The division produced four schools: Education, which took in Educational Studies, Professional Studies and In-Service Teacher Training; Humanities and Social Sciences, embracing English, History, Social Sciences, and Performing and Visual Arts; Sciences, comprising Geography, Psychology, Science, Home Economic Studies and Sports Studies; and, finally, Health Studies.

These changes (UMS, Health Studies and academic reorganisation) readied Urwin for the next stage of the College's development – the first of three she planned. This was to obtain the power to award taught degrees. It would be followed, she hoped, by the grant of power to award research degrees, and then by achieving the grant of the title to make Worcester a university.

The 1991 White Paper had opened the way for a wider range of eligible institutions to be given degree-awarding powers. The plan was to take advantage of that and to prepare an application in 1995 to the Higher Education Quality Council, precursor of the Quality Assurance Agency (QAA), from which such powers emanated. A 1994 quality audit by the HEFCE was deemed by the College as a positive basis for the application. But the plan went slightly awry when, in a subject assessment later in 1994, the HEFCE criticised the handling of music, part of the Combined Studies offering. This was a blow for the College, as Coveney recalled: there had been no clue that anything was wrong from the College's external examiners and 'it made our internal procedures look suspect'. The reaction was to take Music out of the curriculum. In fact, the College won degree-awarding powers for taught courses in 1997, having negotiated the transfer of validation back to itself from Coventry University.

This was an important move. Sir Ron Dearing, in his series of reports for the government, Higher Education in the Learning Society, had recommended in 1997 the grant of university college status to institutions able to award degrees. That fitted Worcester perfectly, so an approach was made to the Privy Council for a change of title. The Privy Council, testing Urwin's patience, as Coveney remembered, took its time, but the Worcester College of Higher Education became University College Worcester, the penultimate move to university title. It capped a fertile period in the College's history, as some self-congratulation in the University College's 1997 curriculum review made clear: 'The rapid development in the last three years of new modules, fields, Higher National Diplomas (HND), Masters level courses and other initiatives, has been the result of considerable academic creativity in the University College.'

The next stage for Urwin was to win the power to award research degrees. This proved such a lengthy process that it became, for her, a piece of unfinished business. Research activity had been at a relatively low level in the 1980s, concentrated in education. From 1994, as Urwin sought to raise the research profile, numbers started to increase significantly.

The National Pollen and Aerobiology Research Unit migrated to Worcester from Holloway, north London, and to this day offers the measurements

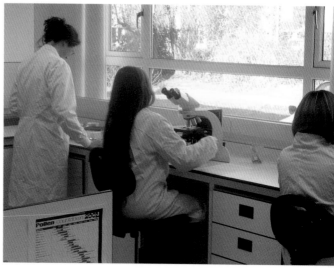

The National Pollen and Aerobiology Research Unit produces the national pollen forecasts, and researches the causes of hay fever and other airborne allergies.

and calculations which help to ameliorate the discomfort of hay fever sufferers around the UK. The Centre for Research in Early Childhood, headed by Christine Pascal, became both a centre for professional study and a respected source of advice for national policymakers. These two units were at the centre of an expansion which saw the establishment of four new research centres between 1996 and 2001. Urwin sought to secure quality and sharpen outside perceptions of the University College among potential postgraduate students by establishing a graduate school, headed by a senior figure with professorial status. Coventry University, which continued to validate Worcester research degrees, gave the University College accreditation in 1999, providing the University College with extensive autonomy to run its own research operations. This, the governors heard, was 'a significant step forward for the University College in its strategic development'. By the end of the

Serving the local community; sixth formers visiting the University College, 1998.

decade, the number of students completing postgraduate degrees, such as Doctor of Philosophy (PhD), was running at eight or nine a year – 'more completions than half a dozen of the new universities', as Bryant observed. The Research Assessment Exercise, undertaken at each institution every five years by the HEFCE, he classified as 'a moderate success'. By the time Urwin left, preparations had begun for an application to the QAA for Worcester to have the power to award its own research degree.

In her first interview with the newspapers after her appointment, Urwin undertook to visit all the further education, agricultural and sixth form colleges in and around Worcester providing education and training for the 16-plus age group. The facilities of the University College must be made more readily available to the community, she said. Her aim was to raise the level of co-operation and collaboration between Worcester and other colleges. This had twin objectives.

The first related to policy. The government, as the 1991 White Paper made clear, was anxious to expand the size of the student population. One way

of doing this in the context of Worcester was to extend the local and regional network of education opportunities. This could be achieved either by offering joint courses with nearby institutions or by making agreements for these institutions to provide foundation courses for potential entrants to Worcester. The collaboration involved in joint courses would maker wider use of the technical expertise in Worcester and other colleges, as, for example, in the 1993 agreement with Herefordshire College of Agriculture to offer a two-year course in Higher Education Environmental Management. The use of foundation courses in other colleges would be a feeder for the Worcester degree courses: one year for the foundation course, leading to entry at Worcester for the remaining years of a four-year educational package. By summer 1993, seven colleges, in Worcester itself and in smaller centres like Evesham and Pershore, had linked up for foundation courses. This provided the University College with a sure stream of entrants, thus strengthening the competitive position of the University College at a time when it was fishing for recruitment in the same pool as 80 universities.

The second objective was financial. The Dearing recommendations would later specify that government funding should follow the students. In other words, low student numbers would mean less funding. But even before that, as the government sought to stem the expansion of higher education, it started to lower the level of funding through the HEFCE. As an element of HEFCE funding to institutions was competitive, there was an incentive not only to maintain quality, but also to exhibit adherence to the broader lines of government

International students celebrating their graduation.

policy, such as widening participation. The HEFCE and the educational institutions agreed a target for student recruitment each year and expected recruitment to stay inside a small percentage band either side of that target figure. If the numbers fell away, then the funding dropped. Not surprisingly, Urwin and her colleagues watched like hawks the trend in applications. The larger the number of students coming from the foundation courses, the better it was for the University College.

There was, however, an area of funding outside the control of the government and its agencies, still ripe for development. This was from overseas. Students from outside the European Union paid full fees, but, of course, they used facilities which the University College already had in place, representing more income with lower overheads, and an enrichment of University College life.

Worcester had overseas links from the days of Ned Peirson, but work to provide a stronger international dimension to the University College gathered force in the mid 1990s, so that in 1997 there were links of various types with 20 other European institutions and 13 US institutions. At their most fruitful, such links led to a joint business

International links have flourished in recent years.

management degree with Halmstad University of Sweden and the presence on the Worcester campus of more than 50 Swedish students.

Overseas activities, like widening participation locally, fitted government policy. In 1999, the Prime Minister, Tony Blair, started a campaign to attract more overseas students to the UK; and the following year, David Blunkett, then Secretary of State for Education and Employment, stressed the need for Higher Education institutions to establish global alliances.

This would not be easy for a college of Worcester's size and position. Eric Jones, in charge of Worcester's international programme, pointed out to the governors in 2000 that the curriculum offered relatively restricted opportunities: Art and Design, Business and Information Technology, Health and Nursing, Postgraduate Teacher Education, Sports and Physical Education. Yet the case of China demonstrated that the University College could achieve modest success in the global market if it concentrated on market niches. It developed a market providing management training for public sector administrators in Chinese provincial governments such as Gansu, Guangzhou and Hubei.

The combination of general recruitment in the UK, the flow of students from foundation courses, the modest success of the overseas effort, and the welcome provided for part-time and mature students, led to a steady growth in student numbers. When Raymond George retired in 1998, he marked the change from the time when he had first become involved with the University College as the chairman-designate of the governors in 1988. At that time, the University College had 1,250 full-time students and a budget of £5.6m; ten years later, it had 3,300 full-time students and a budget of £17.5m. By the end of the 2001–2 academic year, as Urwin departed, there were 3,800 full-time and 2,900 part-time students.

More students produced more strain – on space and money. Although incorporation provided a degree of independence in its financial affairs, the University College, and later the University, remained primarily a teaching institution dependent on public money until such time as it could swell revenue through its own initiative.

Pat Finch explained that the same basic system prevailed throughout the Urwin years and into the 21st century. The HEFCE provided the primary source of funding and based its provision on formulae, which in turn related to student numbers, but the provision was not open-ended: Worcester received a capped allocation of money. The second source of funds was the Teacher Training Agency, deputed by the government in the 1990s to ensure that the supply of teachers matched demand, which worked on the basis of recruitment targets. The third source was the Strategic Health Authority, which provided funds to train nurses. Fourth came tuition fees, of growing importance as the system of supporting students by direct grants from the public authorities ran down in favour of student loans, repayable after graduation.

In each of these cases, the University College obtained funds either for work completed or work to be undertaken. It did not receive public funding to feed its ambition, unless the ambition tallied with what the public authorities wanted it to do. It is true that the body of funding was leavened by extra revenue from foreign students, scattered research contracts and exploitation of the University College estate. It is also true that the HEFCE had various pots of money for capital investment, funds for which colleges and universities could compete.

Worcester relied for the most part on its own resources or on commercial finance for improving and enlarging its facilities. The College financial strategy specified that, out of all the funds received, there should be a surplus of three per cent at the end of each financial year. In that way, the University College could build up its own resources, thus strengthening its ability to attract commercial finance at the most favourable rates. During the 1990s, however, the University College consistently missed the surplus target. Indeed, by 2000, Shadbolt's revenue surplus had been used and the University College had a net debt of £3.2m.

Art studies at Worcester embraces both traditional and modern approaches.

The obvious cause of this turnaround was heavy spending on University College facilities in order to keep up with the growth of academic and training demands. The original wartime buildings required continuing refurbishment. The academic buildings of the 1960s had additions and there was a new building for what had become the Faculty of Health and Exercise Sciences. New residential blocks came in 1995. The library, named after Peirson, was extended by 1996. The University College acquired more sports pitches, on a site of 5 hectares, 3km from the main campus. A new, all-weather playing surface went down within the campus during 1994. By the end of the decade, a new sports hall and refurbishment of the drama facilities had become the construction priorities.

For all that, the University College continued to find space a problem. Urwin, worried about the lack of residential accommodation, tried during 1993 to buy back the land which had given the County Council a windfall just before it lost control of the University College. Negotiations with Fairclough, the housebuilder and owner of the plot, proved, as Urwin told the governors, 'detailed, lengthy and unsuccessful'. The district valuer placed a value on the land of £750,000; Fairclough wanted an additional premium of £620,000, as it sought to recoup a loss caused by buying at the top of the market. The commercial negotiations indicated a gap between Fairclough and the University College of £700,000. 'I judged that it was reasonable to pay a premium of some £200,000 because of the location of the land, but I could not recommend to governors the expenditure of a further £500,000. The cost of the project became unacceptably high and I very much doubt that the funding council (HEFCE) would have approved such an arrangement', Urwin reported.

The library houses a number of sculptures donated by Michael Gibbon. Child with Mother *is carved from ebonized pear wood and mahogany.*

At work in the Peirson Library.

The exterior of the Sports Centre.

Halls of Residence and a student bedroom.

Students in final rehearsals for drama production.

Foiled in the search for extra space, the University College had to concentrate on the existing campus, but that proved only a partial answer. 'Building density on the campus is approaching the maximum desirable', a review of the University College's estates strategy declared in 1999. 'The University College is aware that its remaining open space has important amenity value both to its own community and its neighbours. It is therefore generally intended that any future development will replace existing building stock rather than constituting a net addition to it.' Not that the University College would have been able to decide the future on its own. The nature and scope of campus development came within a development brief worked out with Worcester City Council and revised in 1998. A by-product of that was to push University College and council into closer association on the care of an important asset for the city.

The physical programme took its toll on the University College's financial systems. After incorporation, the University College began to appreciate that receiving and spending money was one thing, but utilising and controlling finance for both the short and the long term was another. Early in the days of the incorporated University College,

the governors advised that there should be an investment strategy which 'should not involve any high risk involvement and only a small portion of medium term risk investment'. This resulted in a move away from the easy system of just leaving funds, immediately surplus to requirements, on deposit at a clearing bank, and towards greater diversity: placing money with building societies, and investing in government stock and in funds specialising in gilt-edged securities.

The greater financial sophistication where existing funds were concerned applied equally to raising money outside the government agencies with which the University College habitually dealt. It started to use its assets as a support for borrowing money in order to create more assets. Financing new residential accommodation proved relatively easy, because this produced income as soon as occupation began, and that income could be used to service loans and running costs. But with facilities like the new sports hall, a mortgage was necessary – in that case, obtained from Barclays Bank with a term of 15 years. But mortgage repayments had to come from any surplus retained from HEFCE funding, or from income from fees and grants. During the 1990s, there was little surplus. Other sources of income – for example, from use of the University College property by outside parties – accounted for less than ten per cent of the University College's total income, which, in 1998–9, came to £19.14m.

By any measure, running the University College's finances meant a tight squeeze. In the late Shadbolt and early Urwin years, there was little experience in the techniques of doing this; that came gradually. John Yelland, the Worcester accountant who joined

Worcester Wolves play their home British Basketball league matches at the University.

University of Worcester basketball team have been University champions for the past three years.

the governors in the mid 1990s and became Chairman in 1999, found the running of the University College finances 'often alien to a commercial approach'. When he was Chairman of the Governors' audit committee, he recalled, 'I delved into the detail. I found no costing, little budgetary control. The College didn't have a Purchasing Officer. Catering was losing a large amount: it seemed impossible to put that right, so it was out-sourced.'

The gradual approach proved a little too gradual when, in 2000–1, 'financial gales blew through the system', as Dick Bryant put it, adding that they constituted 'more a storm than a hurricane'. They started to blow shortly after an evaluation of the University College by the HEFCE Audit Service: 'Our overall conclusion is that management controls at the University College are good. However, there is some room for improvement, for example, in estate management and through further development of audit arrangements.'

In March 2001, as if mocking the first part of the HEFCE assessment, the emergence of a projected £440,000 deficit shocked the governors but made the second part of the assessment look prescient. Six weeks later it appeared that the projected deficit would be £186,000, which was good but confusing news. Then the final outcome was a surplus, somewhat luckily achieved, but a surplus nonetheless.

Behind all this, the governors found out, was a series of unexpected factors. The budget, responding to increased stringency at the HEFCE, had been based on the assumption that salary costs would be 95 per cent of the previous year; it would be possible to make the necessary savings by management of vacancies and reductions in the amount paid to part-time staff. But that had not taken place. In fact, the opposite had occurred. High levels of sickness and maternity leave had increased the need for temporary staff. Student recruitment had been uneven, so more staff had been needed in the buoyant areas, without reduction in the less popular areas. Meeting statutory demands required more staff.

Urwin reacted sharply. She presented a two-year programme. This sought to realign the academic portfolio by cutting out parts of the curriculum for which there was low demand – Women's Studies, Biological Sciences and parts of Environmental Sciences, for example – and putting in place a programme to develop areas of high demand – such as Business, Information Technology, Performing Arts, Media and Social Care. Urwin told the staff that 'costs associated with the current range of academic provision cannot be sustained and that significant restructuring is required'.

In that connection, the University College applied to the HEFCE for over £1m from its restructuring fund, based less on financial difficulties and more on the University College's success in widening participation, increasing educational opportunities for the local community and a strong record both in retaining students and in the students' ability to find employment after their studies.

The other side of the programme aimed to make savings, over two years, of £900,000 on academic staff salaries, £100,000 on non-academic salaries, and £200,000 on running costs outside wage and salary payments. 'Cost savings which have been proposed are in themselves non-negotiable', Urwin stressed. Retirements and redundancies inevitably followed, as the University College lost 30 academic posts, although 14 of these were covered by obliging remaining staff to teach at the maximum nationally agreed figure of 550 hours a year. The cost of redundancies was where the luck came in, in terms of the University College budget. Redundancy costs came to £436,000, but the University College had a windfall of £497,000 as a refund on gas payments. The payment arrived after the financial year-end, but because it applied to 1996–2000, it slid neatly into the 2000–1 accounts, helping to leave the University College with a surplus.

The governors did not want more financial shocks. The way to avoid them, to make certain that there would never again be what Bryant called 'an embarrassing lack of financial information', was for more information to be disseminated more frequently. From early 2002, members of the governors' finance and development committee received monthly reports on income and expenditure, the balance sheet, capital expenditure and cash flow – evidence of the influence of an accountant as Chairman of Governors. Internally, budget holders had to make standard reports and have monthly meetings with a member of the finance office. On top of that, Urwin created a new post: Martin Doughty took responsibility for all aspects of the planning process and the development of a resource allocation model. The University College had adopted a commercial feel.

On 14 May 2002, Urwin had what was probably the climactic conversation of her career at Worcester. Sir Howard Newby, Chief Executive of the HEFCE, the University College's biggest source of funds, paid a visit. Recognising that Herefordshire and Worcestershire did not have the higher education facilities available in most other counties, and that government policy required broader opportunities in higher education, he invited the University College to apply for a major expansion, to 5,000 full-time students, for example. A business plan would be required, but the HEFCE would work with the institution to put together a proposal – in itself, Urwin told the governors, this was 'a significant change in HEFCE's role and its approach to planning'.

Newby and Urwin agreed that the expansion would require a second campus. The HEFCE would support that, Newby said, but under certain conditions. One was that there would have to be a local political commitment and a local contribution of resources: land would be crucial. The second was that the University College should address the needs of Herefordshire.

Here, then, was a potential scheme for enlargement which could run alongside the work

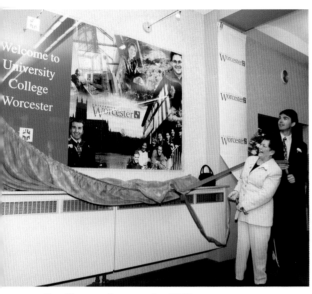

Unveiling a welcome poster, 1999.

already under way to secure university title. Indeed, an outline of the bid for the latter was expected from University College officials just a fortnight after the Newby visit.

Urwin's first call was to Rob Sykes, the county Chief Executive. He proved supportive enough to offer to pay some of the costs of a feasibility study. But before that, the University College needed to decide where it would want to have the second campus.

Doughty produced a memorandum setting out the options – greenfield site outside the city or brownfield site within it – but clearly weighted in favour of staying in the city. The governors saw the memorandum in July and found Doughty arguing that there would be greater potential for unlocking funds from the government and the European Union on a brownfield site. Construction would be cheaper, there would be less duplication of facilities, public transport would be better and it would be easier to maintain political consensus about the project if it was seen to be integrated with the city. This view eventually prevailed, although in mid 2002 it was not immediately obvious where the second campus might be sited.

The problem was resolved towards the end of the year, and Urwin could tell the governors in December that Advantage West Midlands, the regional organisation with an economic development brief, had initiated talks to acquire from the National Health Service the land and buildings of the old Worcester Royal Infirmary on Castle Street in the city centre. At the same meeting, Urwin also circulated the final draft of the application for university title.

This was the last governors' meeting which Urwin attended, and it came with a tribute to her 'extraordinary contribution' over the past ten years, with 'appreciation for her commitment and astute leadership'. But the commitment had a price. Rod Coveney, who worked closely with Urwin, thought that 'in the last couple of years the costs of overcoming a whole succession of obstacles to progress eroded some of her resilience'. Indeed, the pressures had been intense: thin revenue streams, capital cost overruns and changes in the rules on university title.

Although Urwin did not quite achieve her ambition of seeing a University of Worcester under her leadership, she came tantalizingly close. But her legacy was wider than that: the general expansion of the University College, its emergence as the focus of higher educational integration in the region between Bristol and Birmingham, and the higher profile she gave to the University College in the national educational arena. She had been a national figure, on the board of the HEFCE and Chair of the Standing Committee of Principals, a shrewd educational tactician by reputation. Like all her predecessors, she left the College stronger than she found it.

Next page: Art at Castle Street.

Chapter Six

AND SLOWLY EARTH ROLLED ONWARD INTO LIGHT

GREEN, 2003–PRESENT

David Green used a presentation to win the appointment as Dorma Urwin's successor. He set out a vision for 'an outstanding future' for University College Worcester, based on quality, participation and expansion. Attuned to business, a Cambridge economist by training, Green worked in the voluntary and private sectors before embarking on a university career. He ran the business schools at South Bank and Leeds Metropolitan before becoming Pro Vice Chancellor at Thames Valley, where he helped to stage the same sort of rescue operation that Dorma Urwin had achieved at North London Polytechnic in the 1980s.

But Green brought to Worcester a set of qualities complementary to those of Urwin. John Yelland, who worked with them both as Chairman of Governors, observed that 'Urwin was right for the time. When you're building up systems to take an institution to a higher plane, you have to use commercial disciplines. Green is outstanding at strategic thinking. As an economist, he is also very effective on the control of finance and on managing people.' Urwin had been an expert mover in academic circles. Green, who had a wealth of experience in voluntary work, had experience of liaison with the immediate and wider community, and he proved in Worcester that this was important for the University College's broader plans.

Weather vane woodcut from the College magazine, 1947.

David Green, Principal from 2003, then Vice Chancellor.

Just as all the previous principals had brought change, so did Green. He continued where Urwin had left off, taking established themes – expansion, higher standards, heightened efficiency – and reinventing them, to suit both his own approach and the new opportunities opening up in both the academic and the wider environment. The two widest tracks of development, the move to university title and expansion on to a second campus, Urwin had staked out for him.

'The first thing I did was to send out an email asking people to specify one thing they'd like to keep and one thing they'd like to change. I wanted to concentrate on changing, not on re-organising – real change comes from what people are doing rather than structures.' This was Green's first attempt to engage the staff and create an enterprise, both educational and commercial, to which all could adhere. He saw his role as leader rather than manager. 'I tried to create a cross-university focus.' He met the staff – not easy in itself given that by the 21st century the number of staff had risen to 600 – more than double the number of all the people in the College during the days of Hines. Green held regular staff meetings, and encouraged the exchange of news and views by internal email.

Although by 2004 the new University College's strategic plan could claim the existence of 'real institutional elan' and a 'very high degree of staff commitment', Green had the impression when he arrived that the continuum of development needed to enter a new phase. It had the great strength of 'a family and community attitude', but 'people in their work had set their goals too modestly'. In QAA

John Yelland, Chair of Governors, 1997–2007.

reviews of subject teaching, a few departments were proud of scoring 22 out of 24, but none had ever achieved full marks.

For all that, there was a firm base from which to entertain higher aspirations. Indeed, the College (and, later, the University) had a consistent and

Jacqui Smith, Britain's first female Home Secretary, received a PGCE in 1986 from Worcester. In 2005 the University awarded her an honorary degree in recognition of her services to Education and to Worcestershire.

described by the Oxford Dictionary of Opera as 'an especially intelligent, versatile singing actor with a strong dramatic presence'. Peter Terson taught on Tyneside before he made another career as a playwright. Janet Barnett was the 1975 National Dairy Queen. Paul Deneen coupled teaching in Ross-on-Wye with a civic career embracing the chair of the West Mercia Police Authority. Jacqui Smith graduated at Oxford University and then attended Worcester for a teaching certificate before going into politics, becoming chief whip in the last Blair Government and then Home Secretary in the first Cabinet of Prime Minister Gordon Brown. As the scope of the College and University widened, so the alumni have spread into areas unknown to graduates of the original teachers training college. Thus Jenny Burchill, a Sports Science graduate, has devised statistical analysis techniques which are used in sports commentaries to measure performance.

Conscious of the value of this diversity, and anxious to provide courses relevant to a changing society, Green launched preparations for a new University College strategic plan. The process for its adoption included reaching out to other organisations in the region – a notable innovation and greatly assisted by the public standing of some leading members of the University, including John Ryan, the Registrar and Secretary to the Board of Governors, who was also the national President of the Association of University Administrators. Subsequently, a curriculum review, led by the new Vice Principal, Judith Elkin, was directed at quality and content. He saw opportunities across the board: Sports and Leisure, Life Sciences, Business, Creative

creditable record in equipping people of all ages for the professional world. Over 90 per cent of those completing full-time first degrees moved easily into employment. In the early days, of course, the graduate and certificate holders had gone into education: one reason for the strength of the institution in Hereford and Worcester was the spread of the College alumni throughout the schools and institutions of the county and surrounding areas. For example, Helen Ball, Vice President of the students' union in 1957–8, became a distinguished and decorated head in Bristol; and Reverend David Morphy, who graduated in 1971, taught in the county and then became Director of Education for the Diocese of Worcester.

But alumni have shown how a Worcester background can lead into fields unrelated to the individual's original education. In 1973, Clifford Ward, teaching English in Bromsgrove, became probably the first member of the National Union of Teachers to win a place in the pop music charts. Richard van Allan became an opera singer, making a Glyndebourne debut in 1964, and was later

Digital Media through a newly developed centre, health occupations, learning support and early learning. 'I'm convinced there's a great deal of socially worthwhile work to do which will be helpful in terms of income from professional development', Green judged. 'What are the needs of the labour force over the next 20 years? Let's think imaginatively.' This approach was embraced with enthusiasm. Staff creativity brought about such innovations as foundation degrees for future paramedics.

A computing student.

The fashion in which socially relevant and academically secure courses could be offered to students was changing. As the University College reached out into the community and offered more professional development and vocationally apt courses to mature and part-time students, traditional pedagogy – based on lectures, hardback library books and the physical presence of students – needed more flexibility. This came from e-learning, where teaching could be delivered to individual students, instead of the students delivering themselves to the teaching. Students could be remote, yet involved. So the University College moved into what it called 'blended learning', mixing 'the innovation and flexibility offered by electronic delivery with a range of proven and successful teaching strategies'. Blended learning became one way of meeting the government's demands for the national workforce to engage in lifelong learning.

One attraction of new courses for the University College was that often it could use existing assets to provide them. It could receive full income at marginal costs. Imaginative curriculum planning coalesced with existing assets. This was fund-amental. Green told the governors at the first meeting he attended as Principal that 'the underlying

Early Childhood Studies thrives at the University.

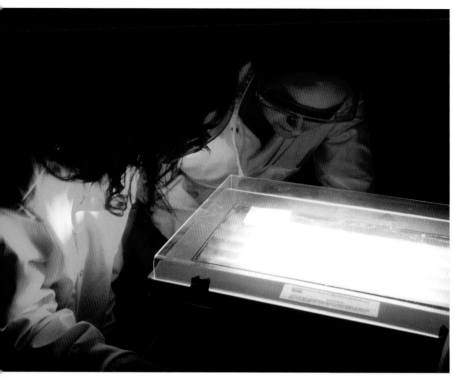

Forensic biology is one of the University's newest study areas.

Students at work on an archaeology field trip.

The Digital Arts Centre boasts cutting edge equipment.

The University's Business School has strong links with China.

income per head than UK or EU students and, in many cases, attend at times when the campus is not heavily used by other students'. The governors were informed that the University College had 30 international students in 2003–4, but sought 75 in 2004–5. The number of students on short courses from China trebled to 120 from 2003 to 2004.

At the same time, Green pushed a policy of making each department generate income through research contracts, consultancy, and so on, with the aim of lifting the overall income per member of staff by 50 per cent in five years. The 2004–5 budget was the first for a new financial arrangement, devolving individual budgets to academic department heads on the principle that cash would follow student numbers and research contracts.

In the sports area, helped by a grant from Advantage West Midlands (AWM), the Motion Analysis Research and Rehabilitation Centre opened as a commercial venture. An allergy testing centre, based on the well-established National Pollen and Aerobiology Research Unit, started business.

Further income would come, Green calculated, from better housekeeping. 'My approach to this campus is to make much better use of our existing facilities.' Halls of residence provided a case in point: with space at a premium for years, it made little sense to have them only 80–90 per cent occupied.

Results flowed through quickly, so that by 2005 the University College had begun to generate investment funds from its own resources. At the

structure of the University College's finances remains deeply unsatisfactory'. Income generation, he added, would be a crucial theme for the University College's Executive Group and wider management. In essence, the problem was that the University College, a relatively small institution, continued to be heavily dependent on the funds it received as payment for actual and future teaching, and did not earn significantly outside them. From this followed a series of moves to create a greater diversity of funding.

More professional development courses represented one direction, of course. Another was to invest in international activity: 'full-cost international students bring significantly higher

Over 2,000 nurses and midwives have qualified at Worcester through a partnership with the NHS.

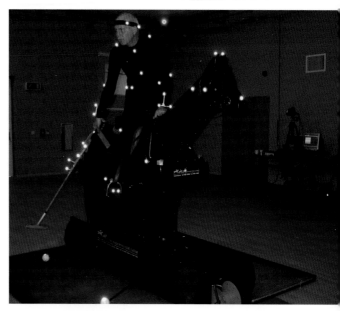

same time, the University College received increased grant income: £9m from the HEFCE in 2004–5, more than it had ever obtained before. Steadily, the College's finances transformed from uncertainty to greater stability – vital for its expansive aspirations.

The University College and Advantage West Midlands (AWM), the regional economic organisation, had first to extract the old Worcester Royal Infirmary from the National Health Service property portfolio. This took until mid 2003, but, once achieved, it opened the way both for the University College expansion heralded in the Urwin-Newby conversation, and for the wider AWM ambition to foster regional economic growth through spreading educational opportunity.

KPMG won a competitive tender to provide a feasibility study, and this brought together for the first time the organisations with an interest in the second Worcester campus: the HEFCE, the AWM, Worcestershire County Council, Worcester City Council, the Herefordshire and Worcestershire Learning and Skills Council, and, of course, the University College itself. They financed the study jointly. The University College 'has engaged key

Work in the Motion Analysis Research and Rehabilitation Centre.

stakeholders in discussion of [its] plans from the outset', observed KPMG.

This was the start of a partnership of many strands. As Yelland pointed out, it is difficult to match up the different ethos of private and public interests. And the project itself was complicated. 'It

Architect's plan showing the new College campus which will create a major cultural centre in the heart of Worcester with its art, performance and conference facilities.

is like building a town in the middle of a city: there are the different elements to fit in, there are buildings to restore, a Victorian chapel to put into context and it's on the edge of a flood plain.' Certainly, the second campus could not be a white elephant. 'It has got to work academically, it has got to work for the community and it has got to work financially.'

The feasibility study established that there would be strong demand for new educational facilities on the campus. The development had 'the potential to create an engine for entrepreneurial growth and higher level skills development' relevant to county and region. The new campus would be a handy 15 minutes' walk from Henwick Grove: down the hill, across the river Severn by the Sabrina bridge and into the city centre.

What the emerging plans for the second campus did not contain until mid 2003 was the original idea which would set it off from myriad urban development schemes. This emerged from the chemistry of internal discussions in Green's management team. It was to create a new library by merging that of the University College with the Worcestershire County Council's public library, to create a centre of learning and pleasure for students and citizens alike. Nothing like this had been attempted in the UK, although there was an example at San José in California.

This proved a practical and elegant proposition. The University College's library needed expansion, and the County Council had been considering moving its library. The idea cut through any notion of educational exclusivity, so it fitted well with the government policy of widening participation in education; it was a natural tool for lifelong learning and it provided a new collaboration with the City and County Councils, integrating the University College further into its community.

No less important for the immediate future of the second campus plans, the library idea gave Worcester a new entry point to capital funding. At first, after the Newby-Urwin conversation in 2002, it looked as if the HEFCE would be able to provide the backing for the sizeable expansion under discussion. A year later, that impression had faded. The HEFCE had run out of funds for student expansion. What it still had, however, was money for approved capital schemes. In January 2004, the University College advanced the idea of the new library. After a series of meetings,

HRH The Duke of Gloucester was installed as the University's first Chancellor in April 2008.

John Ryan, Registrar and University Secretary, 2000–.

Judith Elkin, Pro Vice Chancellor and Deputy Chief Executive, 2003–.

when University College executives fired the imagination of HEFCE officials, the HEFCE agreed to provide £10m. This was the largest single sum of capital assistance that the University College had ever been offered.

The availability of these funds put the second campus project on to another plane. Once finance could be seen to be moving into Worcester, other funds would become more readily obtainable. It was like fitting together the outer edges of a jigsaw: once they were in place, the middle pieces would slide into position. The library required land: the city provided a site adjacent to the old hospital. In turn the Government, through the Department of Culture, Media and Sport provided a large credit for construction. The project had been made safe for the University College: the councils with which it dealt, had made commitments in a joint enterprise.

As Green took over from Urwin, the University College had a twin approach to raising its status: the first was to obtain the power to award its own research degrees, and the second was to obtain from the Privy Council, through the recommendation of

the QAA, the change from University College to University. The two went together because the criteria specified, among other things, at least 3,000 students on degree-level courses – no problem there – and, on the research side, at least 60 current registrations for PhD degrees and a history of conferring more than 30 PhDs.

Worcester's was not an open-and-shut case. Dick Bryant noted that the research story for Worcester was one of both success and failure. On the one hand, the University College had built up a healthy number of research students, who were completing research degrees at the rate of eight or nine a year – 'more completions than half a dozen new universities', he concluded. On the other hand, what he called 'an appropriate research environment' had not been fully created, in spite of the establishment of the graduate school.

Suddenly, the problem evaporated. Charles Clarke, then Secretary of State for Education and Skills, published a White Paper, The Future of Higher Education, which stated: 'We propose to change the system, so that the university title is awarded on the basis of taught degree awarding powers [which Worcester had already obtained], student numbers and the range of subjects offered. This will send an important signal about the importance of teaching, and about the benefits for some institutions of focusing their efforts on teaching well.'

The University College, with its strong focus on teaching, now faced an agreeable choice. There were two main options, according to a position paper which Bryant prepared for the academic board: '1) To continue with the application for university title under current criteria (current indications are that the existing criteria are still in place and that there is still an option to submit). 2) To take advantage of the opportunities set out in the White Paper.'

The paper favoured the second option. The risk of failure had been removed; the University College would have time to address its areas of weakness; application would probably be more straight-forward. Against those points, the University College would have to accept that the claim for powers to award research degrees would be ruled out for the foreseeable future, and it did not know what the new criteria would be, nor what process the University College would have to follow. For Green, the choice was simple. 'To the public University title is everything but research degrees are an internal matter.'

In June 2003, Margaret Hodge, Minister of State in Clarke's department, made public the plans to enable some higher education institutions to become universities, and said that the QAA would be working on new criteria to bring this about. Eight institutions would be eligible, Hodge said. One was University College Worcester.

Worcester moved forward with an application which, as Green informed the governors in October 2004, had been submitted to the QAA, the Department of Education and Skills and the Privy Council as required. The University College turned the submission into a civic and regional event: indeed, at this point, the University College was in a strong position, with student numbers passing 8,000 for the first time, and the number of overseas students attending courses of at least one year reaching 80. John Ryan led preparations for a highly satisfactory audit of College activity from the HEFCE, which buttressed the application.

The QAA conducted its own scrutiny of the University College in autumn 2004. The Worcester application won through. On 8 September 2005, the *Worcester Evening News* celebrated as Green said, 'For the first time I raise a toast to the University of Worcester'. Two months later, University and citizens celebrated in Worcester Cathedral.

The celebrations marked the end of one journey

and the start of another. The journey which had begun in 1946, with one man in a little office, nursing a narrow educational brief, concluded with recognition by the outside world of an important and self-confident institution. The new journey of academic and vocational endeavour in a global economy started encouragingly. Student applications increased at eight times the average rate for UK universities; the expansion of numbers envisaged in 2002 look likely to be achieved by 2009; the expansion of facilities in the £100m second campus development should be achieved early in the next decade. All this would have astonished Hines and delighted Peirson. Fred Grice's telegram in 1946, that the nascent college looked 'chaotic but promising', was half right. Sixty years later, the chaos has long departed, but the promise never left and remains still.

In 2005, celebrations to mark University College Worcester winning full university status which allowed it to change its name to the University of Worcester.

Next page: Graduation day.

INDEX